WALKI

MOMENTS

TALES WITH AN OLD MAN AND A GIRL

SOPHIA TELLEN

Copyright © Sophia Tellen, 2011
Illustrations: Catharine Price ©Sophia Tellen

ISBN 978-1-4092-7614-2

All rights reserved. No part of this book may be reproduced or transmitted in any form or by any means, electronic or mechanical, including photocopying, without permission in writing from the copyright owner.

Published by Tellen Books, Switzerland

To my Muse

CONTENTS

Acknowledgements vii
Foreword...1
1. Uncle Joseph's Good Fortune 6
2. Uncle Joseph Dares to Dare 13
3. Uncle Joseph's S.O.S. 21
4. Uncle Joseph Goes Missing 37
5. Uncle Joseph's Medicine Chest................45
6. Uncle Joseph Drops a Word 62
7. Uncle Joseph's Keys 71
8. Uncle Joseph Breathes into Clay 87
9. Uncle Joseph Obeys His Doctor 98
10. Uncle Joseph Lets Himself be Tempted .105
11. Uncle Joseph Responds to the Moment 112
12. Uncle Joseph Visits His Palaces 122
13. Uncle Joseph Dips into the Fountain 131
14. Uncle Joseph's Tool Box..........................137
15. What's Important is the Rose 147

Acknowledgements

My profound gratitude to Uncle Joseph for his wonderful legacy. He was a gift to Life.

I have very much appreciated the long-term support of two remarkable friends: Pamela Vidal, particularly for her enthusiastic and wholehearted encouragement as she read my stories in all their versions for decades; and Emmanuel Power, whose insightful, incisive, and at times severe editing stretched me and propelled me forward. And who took the photographs.

I am indebted to the Geneva Writers' Group for their helpful suggestions and support, and to the instructors for their dynamism, inspiration and encouragement: in particular Susan Tiberghien, Founder and Director, and Wallis Wilde-Menozzi, the very soul of poetry.

I am grateful to Larry Habegger of Travelers' Tales for his editorial support and advice.

My sincere thanks to Catharine Price, the Swiss artist, who brought her mythical imagination to bear on these stories and translated them into her own magical medium. She is a well-known artist in Geneva.

My heartfelt gratitude also goes to my talented niece, Monique A. Sannes, upon whom I called at the eleventh hour and who arrived like a gift from Heaven, with a panoply of superb skills, to format the manuscript with its illustrations, compose the cover and bring the book to life with her artist's eye.

Likewise, my thanks go to Jim Cooper, whose literary and cultural awareness during the final review enabled me to smooth the remaining rough edges.

I wish to express my sincere appreciation to Melissa Miller, who offered to proofread the manuscript and ended up editing it. Her help was most welcome and proved to be invaluable.

Last, but not least, I would like to offer my deepest gratitude to Dr. Ibrahim Karim (BioGeometry®) for taking the time to read my manuscript and for providing me with additional information about Uncle's pendulum.

Foreword

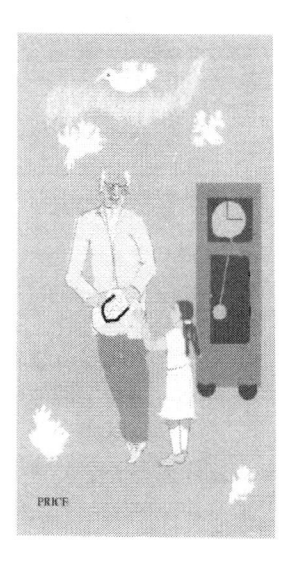

I waited in front of the mahogany grandfather clock, nervously rehearsing my first French words.

We had just arrived in Cairo. My Aunt, in her mid-forties, had come to meet us at the airport. She was wildly excited at having her brother and his three daughters come to visit, as she had no children of her own.

As she opened the garden gate and led us

FOREWORD

along the path, white doves fluttered out of the dovecote and flew up over the garden. The old gardener was squatting on his haunches watering, his thumb pressed over the hole at the hosepipe end to make fine spray.

My Aunt showed my parents and two older sisters to their rooms and asked me to wait in the hall till Uncle Joseph came down. An Egyptian man servant, the *suffragi,* padded by in a red *tarboosh* (fez), a spotless white *galabia* (tunic) and pointed red slippers, carrying a tray of fresh fruit juice.

And then Uncle was there, with spectacles and graying hair. He was seventy, and I was seven.

"*Bonjour Joseph-Oncle,*" I mumbled in awe, getting the words the wrong way round.

At the end of our visit our ways parted and life took us to different continents. We met again briefly three years later when Uncle and Aunt came to visit us in our new home in Cape Town. They took me out of boarding school for the day to celebrate my eleventh birthday with a cake and candles. However, I have no other recollection of Uncle during this time. Thereafter we did not meet again

FOREWORD

for many years.

After living in Egypt for fifty years, Uncle retired in the south of France. For me, too, the cycle ended. Having completed my college education in South Africa, I continued my studies in London. Delighted at my proximity, my Aunt and Uncle invited me to spend my holidays with them on the *Côte d'Azur.* Once there, I would accompany my Uncle on his morning walks, during which he would tell me stories about his life. By then Uncle was eighty-two and I was nineteen.

At first I spent virtually all my school holidays with them. Some of Uncle's stories took place in Egypt, some in the south of France, but he told me most of them in those first two years. The pleasure of seeing Uncle again suffused me. It was a wondrous time. After that I began to travel further afield and would visit less frequently.

Morning walks were moments of delight, as Uncle's presence wove magic into ordinary moments. But with him, one could also encounter the truly unexpected.

Almost fifty years have passed since those walks on the French Riviera.

"Take notes of what I tell you," he had said to me one day, "and you can refer to them

FOREWORD

later." But I did not see why I should.

For decades these memories have lain buried. But quite unexpectedly one day about twelve years ago, while doing some writing exercises, a window opened and I saw them again with startling clarity, as in a film. Then I began to piece together these scraps of memories and weave them into story after story.

When this was done, I found myself trying to retrieve yet one more. There was an event that had long intrigued me, for about it Uncle had been particularly reserved. I tried and tried to extract it from my memory, but to no avail. It continued to float above me like a wisp of curly cloud, but every time I reached up to draw it down towards me, it simply disintegrated.

Finally, in the middle of one night, I recalled some scraps about something scandalous; a few sentences spoken by my Aunt at dinner one day, in a tone of utter disapproval. That was all, and there was no more.

I was about to give up, when early one morning in 2005, on the very day of Uncle's birthday, as I sat at my computer with a cup of coffee, staring blankly at the screen, my fingers suddenly sought the keyboard and

FOREWORD

took off. By the time the clock struck twelve, the elusive new story (*Uncle Joseph's Tool Box*) had arrived, complete! I look upon it as a wink from the Beyond. But as other priorities commanded attention, and my life took its own turn, I began to forget those walks.

Long after his passing, Uncle's birthday remained a special date for me; then I would feel him close to the Earth. I had listened to the Elder with the mind of youth, little understanding the depths of his wisdom; little knowing that the seeds he planted in me would one day take root. And without any idea that I would one day perceive the miracle in the ordinary, and want to pass on his wisdom.

I have tried to present an authentic portrayal of Uncle Joseph, to share his life secrets and to honor his legacy. However, he was a relative who had a long life before I was born, and when our walks began, I was too young to ask the questions I would ask him today.

Sophia Tellen
Geneva, Switzerland
August 10, 2011

FOREWORD

UNCLE JOSEPH'S GOOD FORTUNE

Uncle Joseph was born a hundred and thirty years ago, when trains still ran on coal. The first of five children, he was born on the outskirts of a small town in Turkey. The family was not particularly wealthy, and before he had completed his education, his father went blind and no more money came in. The responsibility for keeping the family now fell on Joseph's shoulders. But first there were exams to pass.

Turkish was the language spoken in the town; but this immigrant family spoke

UNCLE JOSEPH'S GOOD FORTUNE

Spanish at home. Turkish was Joseph's worst subject, and bored him to death. The more he tried to learn it, the less it would go in. So he had no great love for the Turkish language, and the Turkish Teacher had no great love for him. Nevertheless, Turkish was compulsory. So he would open the book at random, pat it down, and begin to stumble through the text. He would do this again and again, slowly and painfully, with dogged determination; all to no avail. No matter how hard he tried, he could not make it stick. Joseph well knew what was at stake, so he would start again and again - disconsolately at times, hopefully at others - only to land in a daydream once more. By the time the exams were due, he had not got very far.

Joseph was intelligent, excelled in all other subjects and wanted to become a teacher. But a good standard of Turkish was imperative, and he feared he would fail. The exam was an oral, so there was nowhere to hide. On the dreaded day the Inspector came to the classroom. He was a tall, broad-shouldered man in his fifties, with greasy black hair flattened against his skull. He seated himself on the dais beside the Turkish

Teacher and, in silence, surveyed the class. Joseph's knees began to tremble.

The Inspector turned to the Turkish Teacher: "I shall now call up one of your pupils to read."

"Certainly, Sir!"

The Turkish Teacher smiled ingratiatingly, sure of himself, either way. The Inspector looked around the classroom with the air of a military commander. There was a deathly hush.

"You there!" he called to Joseph, who had shrunk down in his chair. "Come up here with your book."

The boy clutched his tattered book, and faltered to the front of the classroom. He handed it to the Inspector; then froze. The teacher smiled malignantly, twirling the ends of his moustache. He knew the boy knew no Turkish; no, none at all! The Inspector opened the book, and handed it back to the boy.

The Turkish Teacher said, "Now, Joseph, read nicely to the Inspector."

Then he sat back, exceedingly pleased; *at last* that boy would get his due!

Bone-pale and unfocused, Joseph stared past the open book that trembled in his hands. His head began to hurt. The blood drained into his feet. There was an awesome pause, then, with an effort of will, Joseph focused on the text. He straightened up. Suddenly his voice rang out loud and clear, and filled the classroom. He began at the top of the first page and read without faltering. Towards the middle of the second page the Inspector stopped him.

"Excellent!" he said. "Excellent! You may go back to your desk now."

And to the Turkish Teacher, he said, beaming:

"I must congratulate you! You are a very good teacher indeed!"

The Turkish Teacher's eyes narrowed, and his lips compressed.

Joseph slipped back into his chair.

"But how did you do it?" I asked Uncle, now a youthful eighty-two.

"Chance!" he said, delightedly. "Pure chance! You see, when I began to learn Turkish, I just opened the book at random, and then took the dictionary to try to decipher the text. Not much went in, however. So I would begin at the same page the next time, and the next. So when the Inspector took my book, it fell open at the very place - the only place - I had ever worked at. By the time of the exam, I knew those two pages off by heart!"

Uncle flashed me a brilliant smile.

"I should have failed, of course, but I won a scholarship to a college in Paris instead."

"And what did the Turkish Teacher say?"

"Not a single word!"

As we walked down the boulevard under an azure sky, inhaling the Eucalyptus-scented air in the friendly warmth of the summer sun, Uncle became serious.

"It was bitterly cold in Paris that winter and I became acutely ill. In fact, two of us in the college got the same obscure lung disease. The other student died; but I was more fortunate."

"What happened?"

"I was sent to Egypt."

"By whom?"

"The Director of my College!

She discovered that we had come from the same town in Turkey, although she herself had left much earlier. So she took me under her wing. 'Nathan lies under the ground,' she said. 'I will not stand around and wait for you to die as well. You must leave at once for Egypt; the hot, dry climate will give your lungs a chance to heal.' And she paid for my ticket herself!"

The next day he began the long journey into the unknown.

"When I arrived in Cairo," he continued, "I had no money and had to beg for food. Soon the soles of my shoes had holes in them, and my hat was in two pieces."

I gasped. Uncle had been through all that!

"A stranger befriended me, and sent me to a remarkable doctor. He examined me and said, 'Throw away your medicines, and join the gymnasium. It has an excellent teacher. Take classes with him twice a week and do your exercises every day. Come back to see me in one year.'" Joseph obeyed his doctor.

"I emptied out my bottle of dark liquid, threw out my pills, and signed on at the gymnasium for the *Movement-Cure*. The instructor put me on a graded program and made sure I did the exercises slowly. I attended regularly, and as it turned out, the climate in Egypt was ideal for me."

Gradually Joseph's health began to improve.

"Before long I had so much energy, that after twelve hours' work at the office, I would go back to my room not in the least bit tired, and study till midnight. I had the entire New Thought catalogue of books shipped out to me and read avidly. That's what later led to my first voyage to India."

"You were completely cured?"

"Oh Yes! And from then on I made my life in Egypt, without returning to Turkey. Twelve months later I went back to the same doctor, the one who had sent me to the gymnasium. But when he looked around at the patients in his waiting room, his eyes fell on a young man brimming with health! 'What are *you* doing here?' he demanded. 'There's obviously nothing wrong with *you.*'"

Uncle Joseph turned to me with a playful smile. "It took the doctor a while to recognize me," he said. "I had become a little giant."

The little giant stood 5 feet 4!

UNCLE JOSEPH DARES TO DARE

As new challenges faced Joseph in Egypt, he took stock of his situation.

Dare! he told himself. Make the decision to get out of the impasse. Dare to dare! Audacity can triumph! Act in the Essential. Even *The Absurd* can be essential!

It is early January and I am on holiday with my Uncle and Aunt who live in the upper suburb of a little town on the French Riviera. It is a mild winter's day, and the sun shines brightly, but Uncle puts on his warm coat and gloves. At ten-thirty we set out to cross the boulevard and begin our walk. The black leather caps of his laced ankle boots shine as he places one foot forward after the other. I slip my hand into his and fall in with the unruffled rhythm I know so well, the slow, measured footsteps I love. He walks with grace. We turn toward the blue-green haze of the olive grove, with its low, centenarian trees, their dense, gnarled and twisted boughs covered with oblong pointed leaves whose undersides shimmer silvery-grey in the breeze. As he continues telling his story, Uncle holds me spellbound.

"After a while I found a job sweeping the floor in an office. I was a foreigner, so I was very grateful to be given an opportunity to work. At last I began to earn some money, so I said to myself, I started out penniless, and now I earn two shillings and six pence. That makes me richer than I was by that amount!"

Uncle's voice is grave.

"I decided to put aside ten percent of everything I earned, and did not touch these savings for seven years."

"And what did you do then?"

"I realized that to improve my situation I would need to learn English. So I bought an exercise book, and on its top right-hand corner I wrote the word: Necessity. And I began to teach myself with a dictionary."

"But how could you manage on so little?"

"You see," he tells me calmly, "I had nothing to start with; so I did not even miss the ten percent. Soon I was able to send some money home to the family, and in due time, I even educated my brothers. And after my father's death, I invited my mother to live with me in Egypt.

"After seven years, I had saved seven hundred and fifty pounds. It was not a large sum, but one of the Directors had noticed me. He invited me to start a business with three others. These savings were to be my part!"

In the last year of the First World War, the Spanish Influenza broke out and spread like wildfire throughout the world, killing twenty million people. Joseph, then in his forties, caught it and had to face his second major illness. He survived the acute phase, but it was to take him seven years to get better.

"I was so weak that when my boss called me, it took me up to five minutes to pull myself onto my feet."

A long, harsh cycle had begun. Uncle Joseph became intimately acquainted with illness and came close to death. But he explored alternatives, reclaimed his health, and got married at the age of fifty-eight.

The couple had no children, and Uncle welcomed the visits of his wife's three nieces, of whom I was the youngest. I often came to spend my holidays with them, and it was at such times that Uncle would tell me stories about his life.

Much later Uncle Joseph was to discover the new science of using a pendulum to tune into energy levels inaccessible to the five senses. Identifying and measuring nature's frequencies became Uncle's passionate interest. His pendulum worked for him much like a Third Eye, enabled him to access information about his health, to adjust his energy and restore balance. Thus he was able to maintain harmony and well-being to the end of his days. Indeed, using the pendulum became a way of life.

One mild afternoon that same holiday with Aunty and Uncle on the French Riviera, Uncle invited me to accompany him on a short walk. We turned right, and entered a nearby park. He was happy and carefree, and he began to recall a happening that had taken place in Egypt.

UNCLE JOSEPH DARES TO DARE

"I hired a private train once," he began, with a twinkle in his eye.

"You *did?* And what for?"

"To meet a lady!"

I stared at him in disbelief.

"I had been completely absorbed in my work and was much too busy to think about women, but my Mother kept trying to marry me off. 'Joseph,' she said to me one day, 'you are the most eligible bachelor in this town. You started a business when you were twenty-seven and have been President of the Corporation since the age of forty. And yet at fifty you are still single!'"

Uncle's brown eyes began to dance.

"I was rather timid in those days, but my mother was a most determined matchmaker. Whenever she gave a dinner party, she would seat a suitable beautiful lady on my left. I would converse politely, as with all the other guests, but it never went beyond that. The next day my mother would ask: 'How did you like the young lady?' It never occurred to me that she had been placed there *especially* for me. So, in all innocence I would reply, 'What young lady?'"

His face rippled into an infectious smile.

"But Mother had made up her mind; I was her boy, and she was going to marry me off!"

he continued in a sudden flash of fun. "Once she even invited *two* highly suitable beauties and placed me between them. The next morning she asked me how I had enjoyed the company. 'Thank you,' I replied, 'it was a very pleasant evening.'" He laughed. "I nearly drove my mother to despair!"

Uncle looked back.

"But one day things caught up with me. Your aunt, a young, vibrant Hungarian beauty, arrived in Cairo, and began to give private lessons in gymnastics and free dance. A friend, who knew I was passionately interested in movement, introduced her to me and I engaged her to give weekly lessons at the local orphanage.

"In time I got to know her, and was touched by her youthful beauty and grace. But I was twenty-five years older than she, and so I hesitated; it was to take me seven years to decide.

"When I finally told my mother, she simply said, 'At last!' And, deeply moved, she thanked my fiancée. 'You saved my son from solitude,' she told her later."

His eyes lit up as he remembered.

"But on this particular occasion, I was still single, and I really *did* want to meet a certain lady! She was on a ship from India, docked in

UNCLE JOSEPH DARES TO DARE

Port Said for only twenty-four hours. I had to get there fast. However, just at that very time, the entire country had been immobilized by a train strike!"

"Couldn't you have gone by car?"

"The desert road was too uncertain."

"So what did you do?"

"I hired a private train."

And that train steamed its single passenger non-stop from Cairo – through two hundred and twenty dusty kilometers – to Port Said!

Uncle brought the memory to life.

An elegant ocean liner, a *Castle,* graces the harbor.

A sentinel stands stiffly in front of the gangplank, barring the way.

Uncle Joseph, now President of the Corporation, walks right up to him.

"I wish to board," he says.

"This ship is in quarantine. No one on, no one off, Sir!"

"I have come to board the ship."

"I've got my *Orders!*" retorts the little man. "From *Above.*"

"Still, I *am* going to board."

"Look, my man! No one on, no one off! Have I made myself *clear*?"

"Perfectly!" says Uncle Joseph, taking a step closer. "I'm going up now."

"But what for?" the guard asks petulantly.

"That is no business of yours! Step aside now, please!"

Joseph marches up that gangplank, head held high, and sets foot on the vessel. The lady he wishes to meet is waiting for him.

What they say to each other no one would ever know. But the next day the newspapers proclaim:

> Coup of the Century
> Tycoon hires private train to clinch
> Multimillion dollar deal

Uncle's eyes began to sparkle.

"The reporters even went so far as to declare me the richest man in Egypt. It was pure speculation, of course, for not one of them had the faintest idea what it was about."

"U-n-c-l-e ! *All that* just to meet a *lady!*"

His smile delighted my heart.

"The lady I was privileged to meet was one of the greatest visionaries of the time."

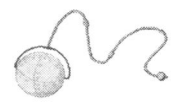

Uncle Joseph's S.O.S.

Retired on the Côte d'Azur, Uncle Joseph lived in the rhythm of peace; peace flowed through every gesture and almost every situation. Hustle and bustle, trouble and noise seemed to slip like water off his back, as he went about his daily tasks in stillness and without haste. His life was rooted in its own order; and one knew what would happen, and when. His best helpers were his wife (Aunty), his psychic adviser (Aymone) and the

UNCLE JOSEPH'S S.O.S.

precious timepiece (fob watch) that resided in his waistcoat pocket, discreetly attached to a fine golden chain.

Each day Uncle situated himself in his small world, and in the larger. There were closed-door times and open-door times. As he began his day, the murmur of his *Morning Prayer* would slip out like balm from his room. Then, according to the needs of the day, he would choose one of his reminder cards: *Patience* (green) or *Keep Smiling* (blue) and stand it on the mantelshelf like a loyal sentry to guard the entrance to his mind. He had had them specially printed, and referred to them constantly. They also served him as calling cards.

Uncle Joseph drew up his horoscope for the week. He consulted it daily, aligned himself with the cosmic energies at play, and lived in the space that lies between cosmic and human time. And yet there was nothing vague about him: his feet were firmly planted on the ground.

After his prayers, Uncle did some of his exercises standing erect, and then lay flat on the floor for his special breathing exercise. "It is very effective for increasing your breathing capacity," he said to me one day. "Lie down on the floor, arms at your side, and start by

UNCLE JOSEPH'S S.O.S.

emptying your lungs through a tiny aperture in pursed lips and push the air out as if whistling, until all the air is expelled. Do this three times. Then, as you raise your arms very slowly by micro movements to a right angle, let your lungs fill up again naturally. Then, keeping the arms still, exhale and then inhale in the same manner, three times. Finally, move to the next position, resting the arms flat on the floor above your head. Exhale again as if by whistling and inhale naturally, repeating this three times. From the floor, through to 180 degrees and back, makes one round. To complete the series, repeat it three times. After practicing for a certain amount of time, you can pass on to the next stage, by doing the same set of exercises holding a small book between your hands. As your lungs strengthen, replace it with a heavier book."

Thereafter Uncle would have breakfast: *biscottes* and tea, with honey or jam and perhaps an apple. Uncle would pop out in his pale-blue woolen dressing-gown, get his morning kiss, deliver one to each of us in return, and disappear back into his room with the trolley. Once dressed, he would do at least an hour's work at his desk. By ten-thirty, he would be ready to go out.

UNCLE JOSEPH'S S.O.S.

Whenever I (a niece) was on holiday, he would invite me to join him on his morning walk. I loved these occasions. As we left the apartment, I would fall in with his pace.

Uncle Joseph was a very precise man in all things, and when it came to human time, his pocket watch was of the utmost importance. There was a hint of timelessness in his gesture as he extracted the watch from his waistcoat pocket and looked fondly at the tapered hands moving against the fine black Roman numerals. It was no ordinary watch, but one with a luminous dial. Day or night, he could always see the time clearly and precisely, down to the last second. This smooth silver timekeeper opened and closed his day; and every night he wound it up meticulously, and set it on his bedside stand, ticking to perfection.

The watch also represented historical time. "I bought it in Austria in the Great Depression," Uncle volunteered one day, drawing it out. "Money had almost no value then. It cost thousands of *Schillings*; but it was still a real bargain."

Once, at the end of my first Easter holiday with my Aunt and Uncle, there was a railway

UNCLE JOSEPH'S S.O.S.

strike in France; trains were few and far between, and there were considerable delays. I had to get back to London where I lived at the time, and we were uncertain as to how to proceed.

Uncle Joseph was passionate in his study of the Unknown, and liked to delve to its very roots. To this end he would meet, twice a week, with a psychic, who had the ability to provide him with precise information, even by means of mathematical formulae.

Now, I knew Uncle had mysterious visits from a lady. I knew, because whatever the season, be it during the Christmas, Easter or summer vacation, every Tuesday and Thursday afternoon Aunty would suddenly banish me upstairs for a siesta! I could not possibly be permitted to disturb him.

But that Tuesday morning Uncle Joseph prepared me. He told me that he regularly worked with a local psychic, who came to see him twice a week. He said that in view of the strike, he would call me in to meet her. Then he would put the matter before her.

When I entered Uncle's room that afternoon, the French windows overlooking the boulevard were slightly open. The light blue damask curtains were lightly drawn aside. The room was fragrant with the aroma

UNCLE JOSEPH'S S.O.S.

of essential oils - now Lavender, now Thyme; now Rosemary or Pine. Uncle was seated at his writing desk, notebook open and fountain-pen poised.

In the low, light blue armchair sat a slender, simply dressed, unassuming woman in her mid-thirties. A deep furrow marked her forehead; her clear blue-grey eyes evoked my immediate trust. Uncle introduced us. Her name was Aymone. Uncle asked: given the train strike, what would she advise? To postpone my return, or to go all the same?

The lady sat still, her hands in her lap. After a moment's silence she looked at me and said,

"It's perfectly safe for you to leave. Your train will arrive on time." And it did!

Uncle Joseph let nothing deter him from the pursuit of his investigations. He inquired into Science and Astrology; color, sound and scent, and matters ordinary or mysterious. Aunty took rather a dim view of all this.

However, at that time she had a particular worry of her own: their old car was in a bad state. Her anxiety clamored to be heard. Uncle Joseph remained deaf to her pleas. But certain of being right, Aunty stood her ground.

So when Uncle decreed that the old

UNCLE JOSEPH'S S.O.S.

banger would have to do for another year, she made up her mind: this, she knew, would require audacity – and an ally!

Without hesitation then, she appealed to Her Own Worst Enemy! Indirectly, of course! And continued to goad her husband till at last he agreed to put the question to the psychic:

Is our old Peugeot still safe?

"No, it is not! Your car has become dangerous!" she replied - short, sharp and clear - much to Aunty's satisfaction!

UNCLE JOSEPH'S S.O.S.

This was not particularly to Uncle's liking, but he agreed to buy a new car – which pleased his wife no end.

Uncle pursued knowledge for the love of it, and delved into the ancient Traditions. He also studied health in its various aspects of body and soul, and in Aymone found an excellent counselor. But whatever the object of his inquiry - be it raising chickens or raising nieces - he could always rely on the psychic to provide the best information.

Long after Uncle's death, Aymone and I stayed in touch. Thus I slowly learned more about her.

Her parents were poor, so she had had to leave school at fourteen to start work. Her first job was in a restaurant.

"Working in that restaurant was sheer hell," she told me. "The heat in the kitchen was unbearable, the pace hectic, the manager unpleasant. We were understaffed, and could barely cope. Then one day a new man arrived, and they made him the washer-up. He worked quietly and efficiently. All day long his hands were in the messy water, sweat pouring down his face, but he worked without complaint. By the end of the day his shirt had got thoroughly dirty. So he took it off and plunged it into the same murky washing-up water that was left after doing the dishes. And when he pulled it out, it was spotlessly clean. I tried to speak to this man, but he did not break his silence," Aymone continued.

I listened with rapt attention.

"I did not know that one day I would have psychic faculties," she said. "My parents were ill and I had to raise my young daughter alone. I had food to eat one day, and none the next, and I was nearly in despair. Then one day I heard a small still Voice within me say: *Je suis là.* I am here. That was all. It was as clear as if someone had been standing beside me. Then there was nothing for the next two years. There had been just those three words, but I clung to them. My psychic development took place later, over many years. It was to be a difficult and painful path and there were many bitter lessons to learn. When my faculties had matured, many people came to consult me, and I had to open an office to receive them."

Aymone worked in a state of direct alertness, without cards or trance.

"Sometimes I receive highly educated clients, who ask questions about matters on

UNCLE JOSEPH'S S.O.S.

which I am totally ignorant. Then I find myself using words I have not heard before. When the client has left, I hurry to the dictionary to look them up. I have never had an opportunity to study and taught myself little by little."

She paused for a moment, then continued,

"You see, it is as if I have four brains. With my right hand I can be writing something down for your Uncle, while my left hand notes an equation. With my third brain I might be worrying about my daughter whom I left alone at home, while with my fourth brain I could be thinking that this armchair is really uncomfortable, and that my back hurts."

Uncle had tested her endlessly over the years, and invariably found her to be right. So the machinations of *The Unseen* were no mystery to him - on the whole.

However, from time to time it was *The Seen* that could be tricky. Sometimes it could even take all of Aymone's inspiration to find the way out of a situation. And *Situations* certainly *did* arise!

One day I phoned Aymone to tell her I had begun to write stories about Uncle Joseph.

"Phone me back next week," she said, "and I will tell you a good one."

31

UNCLE JOSEPH'S S.O.S.

And this is the tale she told:

One day Uncle Joseph lost his pocket watch. He hunted for it, *in*-this and *under*-that, but to no avail. He tried to remember when and where he had last seen it. The only thing he knew for sure was that his watch had been there the day before, and now it had disappeared.

He asked his wife if *she* had seen it; but she had *not*. He asked the maid if *she* had seen it; but the maid had *not*. So, *where* was the watch? And *how* could he manage without it?

Their elderly, heavyset servant-woman was a rare pearl: but full of troubles. She had lived on the *Côte d'Azur* all her life, but had never been to the sea. Her husband had left her, and her son sat in jail; thus she would mutter all day, bemoaning her lot. From time to time she would interject, "Woe is me! Oh! Woe is me!"

When Uncle lost his watch the old servant really felt for him, and was determined to do all she could to help *Monsieur* find it. And so did his wife. Thus the two women conferred, and the two concluded that the watch must be right there, in his room. So, when Uncle Joseph went to the Post Office, the two women moved in and the hunt began.

UNCLE JOSEPH'S S.O.S.

They lifted everything, tossed pillows, sheets and blankets into the air, beat them, shook them and fluffed them.

Then they started on his wardrobe. They dug into the pockets of Uncle's two suits, and rummaged through his shirts, ties, underwear and socks. Nor did the shelf of dried herbs escape their attentions: the women assaulted the brown paper bags of Mint, Lime blossoms, Rose petals - you name it - and something bitter for the liver, something too

UNCLE JOSEPH'S S.O.S.

awful for words.

The essential oils came next. The women lifted and shifted the little dropper bottles of Sage, Thyme, Lavender, Rosemary, Bitter Orange, Eucalyptus and Pine Sylvester. (It was from these that a droplet would sometimes escape, to join the little trail of scented spots that ran all the way down the front of Uncle's dressing gown.)

The women spared themselves no effort. They got into his chest of drawers, his books and his papers. They turned the study upside down.

Only the cream walls and the sky blue carpet were left undisturbed. The more the women delved, the more convinced they became that the watch had to be there. However, by nightfall facts had to be faced: the watch had vanished without trace! And Uncle had lost his smile.

Undefeated, Aunty and the maid set to again next morning, while Uncle Joseph was out. Determinedly they entered the sanctum once more. That watch must be found.

But, it was not!

That afternoon Uncle Joseph remembered Saint Anthony! Well, his private version of the miracle-finder. In his distress, he phoned the Tuesday-and-Thursday lady.

UNCLE JOSEPH'S S.O.S.

Could she help him find the watch?

Aymone listened, and simply said, "Go to the Lost Property Office, the one out of town!"

So Uncle Joseph told his wife, and his wife told the maid.

Then they set off at once, through the dense traffic, past the Railway Station and headed for the Lost Property Office, confident that the watch would be there.

But, it was not!

Aunty exploded.

"This is insufferable! I've always said that listening to *that woman* is a complete waste of time! Sending us out all this way for nothing, and in this traffic!"

Uncle Joseph held his peace.

But by the time they arrived home he was tired out. Back in his study, he let out a deep sigh and dropped onto his bed. He did not land in the middle, as was his wont - but somewhat higher up. In fact, he landed on his pillow.

The poor man was so worn out that now even his soft pillow felt hard. He reached down to look for the source of the trouble. As he did so, his hand brushed against something solid, and before he could grasp what had happened, his fingers closed around

UNCLE JOSEPH'S S.O.S.

the slim, smooth silver timepiece! His pocket watch had been shaken into the depths of the inner flap of the pillowcase, and had got stuck there.

The next morning Uncle Joseph phoned the psychic.

"I found my watch."

He heard her heave a sigh of relief.

"But *not* at the Lost Property Office!"

Aymone felt herself going cold all over. How *could she* have made such a mistake! How *could she* have sent the man she revered as her Teacher so far out of town – and all for nothing? Berating herself thus, she begged the Venerable One to forgive her.

"No! No! No!" replied Uncle Joseph, emphatically. "It was no mistake at all!"

Aymone was beside herself.

*Oh! How could he! How could he!
And with all the depths of his honesty!*

"But *Monsieur,* how can you say such a thing, when you *know* I misled you?"

"The answer you gave me was perfect," he replied. "For, you see, *it had to stop*! The moment you told me to go to the Lost Property Office, I told my wife and she told the maid, and the whole commotion came to an end!"

Aymone stood at the other end of the telephone line. As she reached the end of her story, I could almost *hear* her smile.

"And there you are!" she concluded.

"That night, your Uncle found his watch right under his backside!" She chuckled.

"I love to tell this story," she continued, "for it shows your Uncle's attitude towards The Absurd. You see, things had got completely out of hand. In the ensuing impasse a special kind of action had been required. Your Uncle called this: *The Act in the Middle!*"

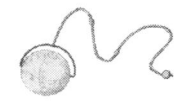

UNCLE JOSEPH GOES MISSING

It is ten-thirty and time for our morning walk. I hang around Uncle's closed door, hoping it will soon open.

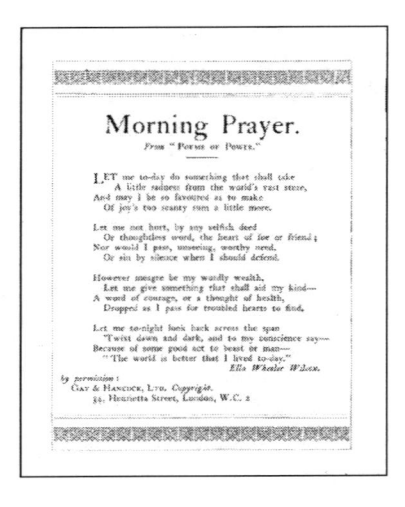

> ## Morning Prayer.
> From "Poems of Power."
>
> LET me to-day do something that shall take
> A little sadness from the world's vast store,
> And may I be so favoured as to make
> Of joy's too scanty sum a little more.
>
> Let me not hurt, by any selfish deed
> Or thoughtless word, the heart of foe or friend;
> Nor would I pass, unseeing, worthy need,
> Or sin by silence when I should defend.
>
> However meagre be my worldly wealth,
> Let me give something that shall aid my kind—
> A word of courage, or a thought of health,
> Dropped as I pass for troubled hearts to find.
>
> Let me to-night look back across the span
> 'Twixt dawn and dark, and to my conscience say—
> Because of some good act to beast or man—
> "The world is better that I lived to-day."
> *Ella Wheeler Wilcox.*
>
> by permission :
> GAY & HANCOCK, LTD. *Copyright.*
> 34, Henrietta Street, London, W.C. 2

I have heard the murmur of his Morning Prayer. I have heard him sound the tone of the day: a single, solitary sound, different each morning. I can't wait for him to emerge.

But today he is held up. He has had to deal with urgent business. At ten past eleven he emerges at last, impeccable in his white shirt and tie, and double-breasted suit. Its blue is lighter than navy, with a touch of teal in it, perhaps also grey. His face is smooth and oval, without wrinkles. A toothbrush moustache graces his upper lip. In the little hall Uncle puts on his coat and reaches for his grey hat. He extracts his walking stick from the brass umbrella stand. Its wooden handle shines; it has served him well. He puts on his gloves and we are ready to depart.

We close the front door and leave the apartment together. Aunty is glad to see us go. She is fiery and fleet-footed; Uncle's pace is slow. In her sixties, she is slender, and has retained her youthful beauty and vigor. She needs the windows wide open; he feels the cold. She gets up at the crack of dawn, does her exercises, is at the market by six, haggles for fresh fruit and vegetables, and is back before anyone is properly awake. She is twenty-five years younger than Uncle, and marvelously fit.

Aunty loves outings and could keep going tirelessly. Her brother is only a year and a half older than she, but once when she took him on *a little excursion* into the Maritime Alps to show him the region, she wore him out on a regular five-hour march.

We take the creaking lift, descend two floors, emerge from the foyer and set off on our walk. With old-fashioned courtesy Uncle doffs his hat to a lady as we pass. She is even older than he.

Uncle is small, thin and frail. His hands are often cold, especially in winter. I slip my left hand into his right, and adjust my pace. He stops and looks to the right and to the left, and once more to the right, and we begin to cross the boulevard.

Suddenly his hand tightens on mine.

"This is where I got run over," he says, as his walking-stick touches the white line in the middle of the road.

"How did it happen?"

"No car was in sight, so I began to cross. Suddenly a motorcycle appeared at the top of the hill and came hurtling towards me. I stopped here, on this white line, leaving him plenty of room to pass on either side. But the reckless rider rode right into me!"

(Aunty had written to us about his accident. It had taken Uncle a long time to recover.)

We walk under the swish of the Eucalyptus trees, whose ragged bark is peeling. We left late today and there is a steady rumble of traffic on the boulevard. Uncle turns left into a side street. We pass ochre houses and gardens fragrant with Bougainvillea bushes in bloom and Wisteria.

Somewhere behind us a car exhaust backfires like a shotgun. It is a quarter to twelve. The traffic on the boulevard is already intense; and even in this side street I can hardly hear Uncle speak. The rasping mopeds, with the long, crisp loaves of French bread sticking out of baskets or bags on back-racks, are the worst. Hooters blast as cars rush by to get home for lunch.

"Uncle, let's go back! It's too noisy today."

Blood rises to his head. With iron-hard determination, he swings back into the pounding midday traffic of the main road. I am obliged to follow.

"Let's go back," I insist. "This din is getting on my nerves."

Uncle reins me in sharply. His tone is fierce.

"No!" he snaps. "I do *not* accept that! I refuse to be governed by nerves: yours or anyone else's! I am *not* prepared to let mere traffic noise curtail my walk."

I am stunned.

"I do *not* have to shrink away! This noise does *not* get on *my* nerves."

With the thump of his cane on the

UNCLE JOSEPH GOES MISSING

pavement he pounds the words into my head.

This is a new Uncle; one I do not know. The mild man has turned into a lion. He strides up the boulevard, tugging me along as if I were a child.

Eyes flashing, he turns to me once more and proclaims: "I refuse to believe I can*not* this, I can*not* that, because *its-getting-on-my-nerves*! I am *not* too sensitive to stand the noise! I can! I *can!* "

However, the truth is, Uncle was extremely sensitive, although he never referred to it. One day he related the following incident with an amused smile.

"I was sitting in a lecture one evening, when I suddenly felt a violent pain. I shifted my position, but nothing helped. I did not know where it came from or what to do. I turned to the man sitting beside me and whispered, 'I don't know what has hit me; my right leg hurts as if it had been amputated.' And he replied, 'Well, *my* right leg recently has!'"

Back on our walk, Uncle quickens the onward pace; it is the only time I have ever seen him do so. Cars honk without respite as people make their midday dash for lunch.

We return in icy silence.

UNCLE JOSEPH GOES MISSING

A few days later Uncle Joseph disappears. He *was* with us at lunch; we all saw him. Then he went to take an afternoon nap. At four o'clock his door is still closed. Theirs is only a small flat, but Aunty cannot find him anywhere. (We are about to witness a spot of theatrics!)

"He's gone!" slips out in dismay. "What if something awful happened to him?"

Aunty sends me up to the attic to see if her husband has gone to fetch something from his blue leather suitcase; then down to the basement. He might have gone to get some wood. She rings the doorbell at the neighbors - the one on the right and the one on the left - but *désolé,* they have not seen him. Neither the one, nor the other!

"Run to the Post Office," she says. "He might have gone to buy some stamps." I head for the door. "And pop in at the greengrocers' while you're down there, and ask Jacqueline. Jacqueline always knows everything. If not, stop at the *boutique.* The owner is a friend."

I dash around and dash back. But no! Jacqueline has not seen him; nor has the owner of the Boutique. I tell Aunty, "No one has seen him!"

UNCLE JOSEPH GOES MISSING

"Now run the other way," she says. "Try the Tobacconist's; he could be there."

But no, he is not!

"C'est une catastrophe!"

My Aunt is at her wit's end, and just about drives me to mine. Her Joseph has vanished, without trace!

"What if some evil has befallen him?" she asks in a voice of tragic doom.

Then: "Run to the Chemist across the road. Joseph might have gone to buy a camphor stick for his sore neck."

But no, Uncle has not been seen there. Nor anywhere! Aunty is in despair. We meet again in the dining room. She starts throwing up her hands heavenwards, fingers spread-eagled, as if to ward off this evil thing, but they stop, startled, at each side of her face. Suddenly the key grinds in the lock and the front door opens slowly. Uncle Joseph walks in. Aunty rushes up to him.

"Oh! Papi! Papi!" she cries out, falling around his neck.

"Whatever is the matter?" he inquires innocently.

"I thought we'd lost you!"

Joseph, the Untamed, looks years younger.

"But *where* have you been?" Aunty calls out. "I was worried to death!"

"*Sapristi!*" The word slips out like a schoolboy's whistle.

"I was only up the road at the Barber's!"

Uncle Joseph raises his hat to reveal the neatly trimmed semi-circle of grey hair nestling around the shining dome.

Then, with the merest hint of a smile, he slips back into his study and closes the door.

Uncle Joseph's Medicine Chest

"This man," Aunty exploded, "could keep a whole harem busy!"

She was complaining about her husband. All the washing had to be done at home, even though they had no washing machine. He wanted dinner served on a white tablecloth, like it always used to be! In Egypt, that is. But n*o, no, no!* The plastic cover was going to stay! Having a wife and a maid was not enough: now he had to rope in *her* young visitors as well!

My school friend, Pamela, and I had arrived from London, and were on a short holiday with Uncle and Aunty. We were sitting around the circular table in the dining room, helping Aunty sew silk hats for Uncle Joseph. She had machined the greater part of them; now we had to hem them by hand. There were two hats in each color of the rainbow, together with black and white. The silk threads we used were lovely to look at, and a joy to work with. The two of us were relaxed and having fun. But Aunty was raring to take us out; there were such interesting places she wanted to show us.

For healing, Uncle used plain squares of

colored cloth; he had two sets of the spectrum, in wool and silk. (Each square could be used only once; thereafter it had to be both washed and ironed). He also had seven silk kimonos, and seven little hats. The old hats had worn out, and it was these that we were replacing.

Staying healthy was for Uncle Joseph a conscious, ongoing process. He had been examining the various ways to maintain health for several decades, and this included long fasts. (In Egypt, he had devoted the whole upper floor of his house to drying herbs).

But staying healthy took a lot of time. (Especially *hers*, Aunty thought, and occasionally *said!*) Uncle Joseph had his own version of where time went.

"Love is all very wonderful," he said one day with a delightful smile.

"But being married takes up a lot of time!"

In the course of his studies Uncle discovered an ever-changing two-hour correspondence between colors, the tones of the scale and the hour, and drew together color, sound and time in a neat chart.

To sound a tone he would blow into a

chrome-colored metal pitch pipe, a small tuning instrument with a pointer and a flared, adjustable end-piece marked with the scale: *Fa So La Si Do Re Mi Fa.*

Up at the crack of dawn on a Friday? You will find yourself entering indigo! Attune yourself by toning *La*! Work late on a Wednesday, and you will be immersed in sky blue till midnight. Tone *Si*, or put on your colored hat, for extra mental stamina! Hum *Do-Re-Mi* on a Saturday from noon to six, and you will be moving through red-orange-yellow as the week draws to a close.

Each essential oil also has its matching

UNCLE JOSEPH'S MEDICINE CHEST

color. Increase your meditation power with violet from four to six a.m. on a Monday with a drop of Verbena or Rosemary, or treat yourself to indigo with a drop of pine essence at the same time on a Friday. Stuck in the city? Enjoy the feel of green with a spot of cypress oil on your wrists at ten a.m. on a Thursday, or once more in the closing hours of Sunday!

Uncle Joseph had never studied at a University, but had educated himself. He further developed his knowledge by studying the works of two French scientists, Léon Chauméry and André de Bélizal. They called their science *Microvibrational Physics*, to differentiate it from the practices known as Radiesthesia in Europe and as dowsing in England and the United States. He learned that all things in the universe have an energy field, vibrate and are interconnected and can be measured. By the time I met him again as a young adult, Uncle was a skilled practitioner with over twenty-five years' experience. This science enabled him to experience himself as part of the energies of nature and gave him the ability to change things. Uncle Joseph was an old man who had acquired the power of

UNCLE JOSEPH'S MEDICINE CHEST

knowledge.

Uncle also loved to experiment. His Chauméry pendulum, a scientific device that could not only detect but also emit energy, enabled him to tune into an unperceived world, capture its ever-changing patterns and place himself in harmony with them. Using a color scale of measurement, this pendulum enabled him to undertake some fascinating research. For instance, Uncle found that for two hours each day, plants have a *high* time.

"Have you ever noticed a particular patch of flowers or a bush that suddenly stands out as vividly as if it had come alive? Then that is *its hour*."

One day at lunch I asked Uncle to teach *me* how to use the pendulum.

Beside herself, Aunty snapped: *"Pas question!* Not on your life! One in the family is quite enough!"

Next holiday a stomach-ache sent me to Uncle. He said, "I shall show you how to help yourself."

He fetched a pile of colored Viyella squares and spread them out on his bed.

"Hold your arms out above these squares of cloth and close your eyes. Now let your hands sweep over the colors. Stop when you feel anything." I did as he instructed.

"Here it feels warmer," I said, surprised.

A wave of pleasure rippled across his face.

"Good. Now continue. Is there another place where you can feel anything?" There was.

"You have done well," he said. "Yellow is for the liver, and green is good for your stomach. Practice and you will not need a pendulum."

After a moment's thought, he added: "It would be helpful for you to have a blouse of every color. In the morning, before you dress, slip your hand into your wardrobe and let it land naturally on a color. Then that will be the one you need to wear. A woman can easily harmonize her energy that way. And it would make you feel really good, too."

In those days I often got exhausted for no apparent reason (*your batteries get depleted too quickly,* he said) and would ask Uncle to help. Then he would take his pendulum and adjust it for the task in hand. It is a sphere, a boxwood replica of our globe (five centimeters in diameter) with a movable copper arch mounted at the poles, to which is attached a string with three knots (holding points); the first representing the electric meridian; the second, the magnetic, and the third, the electromagnetic equator. The instrument swings back and forth or gyrates (clockwise or anti-clockwise) at different speeds, thus providing clear information in answer to simple, direct questions.

Uncle would ask me to face North, measure the frequency of my body's peripheral energy field (*take my note*) and seek the cause of the disturbance. Then he would let his free hand hover over the dropper bottles of essential oil on the middle shelf of his wardrobe, observing the rotation of the pendulum till it had indicated two remedies. After which he would put one of the *magic* drops on my left wrist, and another on my right. "Now rub your wrists together till the essences are absorbed and lie down for ten minutes." The drops nearly always worked well. However, on rare occasions they would make no difference. Then Uncle would say, "Ah! This requires stronger measures!" Thereupon he would consult one's horoscope and after a moment murmur, *"I see!"* Whereupon the next two drops of essences were bound to make one feel much better.

There was something unfathomable about Uncle. On the chest of drawers, beneath the small wall bookshelf in Uncle's study, stood a truncated pyramid, open at the top, made of stiff card and nine inches high. If one was feeling particularly dreadful, he would place one's photo inside it for several days.

That pyramids were of particular importance to Uncle Joseph became clear one day, when at the end of one of our morning walks he suddenly said, "I spent one night alone in the Great Pyramid." But thereafter he fell silent and never referred to it again.

Sometimes, according to some personal need, Uncle Joseph would immerse himself completely in a particular color. One evening, at ten o'clock, I knocked lightly at the door of his room to say good-night. As I gently pushed it half open, the fragrance of blended essences wafted towards me like the perfume of Heaven.

But I stopped short at the threshold. An apparition was seated at the desk deeply engrossed in work. It did not at first look up. A band of silver glinted against the black resin of the poised green and white striped fountain-pen. A violet silk hat crowned the bent head poring over a barely visible hand, writing. Slowly it dawned on me that the figure draped to the floor in a violet kimono, was that of my Uncle. It was like walking in on a Mysterium!

UNCLE JOSEPH'S MEDICINE CHEST

As the years rolled on, Uncle Joseph remained fully alive and alert. Nor did I even once hear him say that he was tired. Able to decode the energies around him, to correct or transmute them, he kept himself in tune with the moment, realigning himself as he went along. Walks were no exception. He would start out in one direction and never return the same way if he could avoid it, 'because new energies can always be gathered on a different route.' One day we went for a long walk in a forest. Uncle said, "If you feel exhausted, sit on a tree stump. Its rising energy will revitalize you."

For extra vitality Uncle had a set of colored paper squares for his shirt pocket. Thus he might place a patch of indigo over his heart. He also had a stamp-sized set to tuck into his boots, under the soles of his feet. Thus equipped, he would set out for his daily walk. These little rectangles of colored paper mostly stuck to his socks. However, on occasion, they would work their way up the heel, creep up his boots - up, up above the laced-up ankle - and out, leaving behind him as he walked along, a tell-tale trail of tiny colored markers.

Aunty railed: "I'm just waiting for the day when some old crone will sneak up to me

UNCLE JOSEPH'S MEDICINE CHEST

with sly satisfaction to announce: 'Ah Madame, *your* husband will never get lost!'"
If Uncle readily dispensed his "magic" for the mere price of being asked, he was not – we were to discover - past dispensing a little of it into his own life, too!

One day, with a sparkle in his eyes, he said, "I need a narghile. If you ever happen to go to Turkey, please bring me one."

Bring Uncle a hookah! The mystic water pipe?

Oh dear! Was he going to start smoking now?

55

UNCLE JOSEPH'S MEDICINE CHEST

"The narghile," I read, "gives pleasure to a special breed of smokers."

Aha!

An impish thought intruded. So what kind of a breed was Uncle? Was he hoping to return to his Ottoman past? Or hankering after some secret world in Cairo?

Of course, the *special breed of smokers* referred to one of the oldest traditions of the Middle East, *hookah* smoking in the cafés and on streets, with the unhurried sharing of stories and ideas. But China, Turkey, Afghanistan, Iran and India also enjoy the narghile, smoked by both men and women alike.

But to bring back a narghile! And from Turkey! I would have done anything for Uncle, but at that time a trip to Turkey seemed about as likely as travelling to Venus.

Just six months later, I found myself on a cruise around the Greek islands – a 21st birthday gift from my best friend, Pamela. Our boat would take us from Piraeus to Crete, Rhodes, Kos, Patmos, Mykonos and Delos. On the third day there were to be a few hours at Bodrum, just fifty minutes by ferry from Kos (or today, twenty minutes by hydrofoil).

When St. Peter's Castle loomed ahead, we could not linger. Somewhere behind these ruins was a narghile!

Armed with youthful determination, and in a spirit of adventure, we made our way directly to the mysterious Old Town, with its labyrinth of small shops tucked into narrow streets that wind around an ancient plane tree, and straight into the lure of beautiful hand-crafted goods — sandals, carpets, silver ware, jewelry and ceramics - followed by the keen stare of male eyes. We stopped at one shop after another, calling out hopefully, "Narghile? *Hookah?*" — Without, however, seeing a single one! Overwhelmed by the glittering opulence of the wares, and the enticement of the salesmen, we would surely have got lost in the maze of alleys and possibilities.

Suddenly a deep, friendly voice behind us addressed us in English.

"You should not be walking around here alone!" (Later I discovered that we were probably among the first female tourists they had ever seen).

We spun round. A tall, bearded and weather-beaten man looked at us, clearly worried. "I'm Jason," he added.

"We are trying to buy a *hookah*," said Pam, and as if to emphasize the veracity of this unlikely fact, she added, "It's for my

UNCLE JOSEPH'S MEDICINE CHEST

friend's Uncle! However, we don't speak a word of Turkish," she said with a grin. "And what are you doing here?"

"I work here," he replied, "and have been in Turkey long enough to learn the language. Would you like some help?"

I looked at Pam doubtfully. A year older, and always self-possessed, she considered the matter. Taking things in her stride, she looked at her watch. Time was short, and so far we had got nowhere. Finding a *hookah* for Uncle was not going to be as easy as we had hoped. She searched my eyes for acquiescence. Then, composing herself, she said on our behalf, "Thank you. That would be great!"

Jason's enquiries soon led us to a tiny shop that sold *hookahs*. Âs we stood outside, the salesman smiled and invited us in. Courteously he handed each of us a dainty glass of sweet apple tea. Then he showed us the different hookahs. They were of copper (altogether hand-made), brass (easier to work than copper) and nickel, and had glass bowls. However, there were a few made entirely of metal and less fragile. Several were elaborately decorated.

"Bargaining is a tradition here," Jason said to us. Turning to the salesman, and pointing to a decorative *hookah*, he asked,

"How much is this one?" and was given the first price in old Turkish Lira (a million of which equal one new Lira today).

Jason's brow furrowed into a deep frown.

"No, thank you," he said. "And this one?"

While he looked disinterested, we tried to fathom out which narghile to buy and decided Uncle would want a simple, economical model. "What about this one?" I asked. This narghile was made of nickel and twenty-one inches tall.

"This is the best of its kind," said the salesman. "Guaranteed!"

"But does it *work?*" asked Pam. Jason translated.

The salesman raised his eyes to Allah! We were the first customers of the morning, and he was sure of his luck.

"Under the Heavens," he boomed, "every honest citizen would be happy with it! Just look how well each part is made."

He began to dismantle it. There were four main parts, beginning with the clay bowl at the top (for charcoal and tobacco) sitting on a centre piece, which went all the way down to the hollow, hand-blown, glass vase to be filled with water.

"Just look at this long, leather hose and

mouthpiece. Any man would be proud to use it," the salesman continued.

Lovingly he handled each piece and began to fit the narghile together again.

"Each part is made separately by an expert craftsman. I can give you the special tobacco for it too," he continued. "Tobacco that has been soaked in fruit shavings, such as Double Apple (red and green), Red Apple and Peach. This mixture is smoked through the large water pipe, while the water cools the smoke."

Jason looked concerned, obviously wondering whether the *hookah* would ever work again.

"I'm a deep sea diver," he proclaimed in a voice that rose from his belly. "From Canada! And have learned to see into the depths of the sea."

Tall as he was, he frowned down at the shorter man.

"And I will take nothing less than the perfect *hookah*!"

Jason made as if to leave. We turned to follow him.

"But Sir, Sir!" the salesman called out urgently. "You could not buy a more perfect article. And look at the price! I will reduce it just for the young ladies."

Jason broke into a smile. "Well," he said,

UNCLE JOSEPH'S MEDICINE CHEST

turning to face us, "what do you think?"

We nodded in agreement.

I handed the salesman five crumpled notes. We shook hands on it, and left the Bodrum Old Town with the blessings of the salesman and the good wishes of the Canadian.

The last obstacle was to make sure I got the *hookah* safely to Uncle. I wrapped all my clothes around it and put it into my travelling bag. At the end of our cruise I returned to Piraeus and took the train, while Pam continued to Sicily. I tucked my bag under the seat, and kept my feet protectively over it. There were changes to negotiate. I fell asleep on the long, long journey up the boot of Italy, waking up with a start every now and then to feel my treasure. Finally I reached the south of France. As the train whistled to a stop, I extracted the heavy bag, and made my way to Uncle's door.

"We found you a narghile!" I announced with quite some pride, presenting *The Find* to Uncle Joseph, while Aunty simply could not believe we had actually bought it in Turkey.

Uncle examined it carefully, remained silent, then thanked me courteously.

"What did you pay for it?" he asked.

(It was only a fraction of what a narghile

costs today).

"That seems perfectly reasonable," he said, rising to refund me. (Currency conversion was a child's game to Uncle).

"Well, do you like it, Uncle?"

Eagerly I awaited his comment.

"It is very decorative," he said at last.

My heart sank.

The sinking feeling stayed. The return trip to London felt dull and flat.

It was with quite some astonishment, therefore, that a month later, I received a letter from Uncle with the following postscript:

"A pleasant surprise that will surely make you happy: It has so turned out that the narghile I thought was just a toy, not only works very well, but I am finding it useful for breathing exercises that, according to my health counselor, will help my bronchi. To replace the tobacco, I put some essential oils on cotton wool. Then I breathe in the "magic" essences. What a pity that you are not here to see the Pasha use his narghile every morning!"

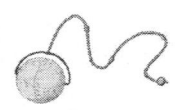

UNCLE JOSEPH DROPS A WORD

Uncle's pendulum was always with him. At meal times it would lie like a silent witness beside his plate, or act as counselor.

But Uncle also had a number of other unusual remedies.

One day at dinner, Aunty and I began to discuss the ideal diet.

"What do you think about all this, Uncle?"

"There is no universal formula," he replied. "A diet that suits one person is not necessarily good for everyone alike. Every individual is unique. One cannot treat people like test tubes in a laboratory, nor put into them x, y, z and expect the results to be the same. Get to know your body. Then you will find the diet that suits you best. But far more important than what one eats, is that one chew it well."

And he began to tell a story.

"Your Aunt and I once met a lady during a holiday in Bretagne. She had innumerable ailments. She had gone from doctor to doctor to doctor, and had consulted specialist after specialist. She had taken all kinds of pills; tried all kinds of diets; been to several spas; but she got no better, not a whit, not a bit.

UNCLE JOSEPH DROPS A WORD

Her husband had devoted his life to looking after her, until finally he died, leaving her alone with all her miseries. Convinced she was incurable, she became depressed."

Intrigued, I asked, "So what happened then?"

"She came to me one day in despair and asked, 'What else is there for me to try?'"

"Stop looking for yet another doctor, I suggested. Drop your innumerable pills and eat whatever you like. Take a bite, put your fork down, and think of something funny. Then take another mouthful and chew until it becomes liquid. Put your fork down once more, and tell yourself a joke. Keep this up to the end of each meal."

She stared at me in amazement.

"Do this every time you eat and you will soon feel better."

Uncle Joseph paused and smiled.

"Thereupon our ways parted and we lost touch; nor did we imagine that we would ever see her again."

Uncle Joseph's magic came in small packages. He never preached or told others what they should do; nor did he ever *offer* his help. However, if anyone *asked* him for help, he

UNCLE JOSEPH DROPS A WORD

gave it willingly, for he had learnt much during the course of his life, had been close to death three times, had outlived the danger, survived a number of storms and squalls, and reached the age of ninety-four.

His home pharmacy held a few simple remedies: the odd salve, a bottle of Dettol, the age-old British disinfectant, some magnesium chloride and sodium bicarbonate. Uncle knew how to enliven these with his pendulum, and could lend them much greater efficacy.

Once a week Uncle took a warm bath to which he added a cup of bicarbonate of soda. (Aunty always bought five kilos at the *Droguerie*). This bath is a sheer miracle. In fifteen minutes it will cleanse, refresh, deodorize and soothe. Even at his age, Uncle's skin was smooth and fresh.

Aunty does not particularly appreciate *all-these-goings-on-with-the-pendulum*, but she is the first to turn to him when something has gone wrong. Once, Uncle's use of this instrument helped her get rid of a prolonged toothache.

"Put five drops of Dettol into half a glass of lukewarm water, and take a mouthful. Hold it

UNCLE JOSEPH DROPS A WORD

for thirty seconds and rinse. Repeat this three times in a row, and five times during the day." Forty-eight hours later Aunty's toothache had disappeared.

Like my father, my oldest sister is an engineer; like him, she's very logical. Like Aunty, she does not believe in *all this nonsense*. But one year her face broke out in ugly spots. By the time she arrived on holiday, the spots had been there for weeks. So she said to herself, "I'll consult Uncle Joseph! It can't do any harm!"

And went to him with her problem.

Uncle calibrated his instrument and oriented her for this investigation.

"Face the wall," he said, pointing to the North. "Now hold out the palm of your right hand."

He let the pendulum rotate above it, until he had identified her personal energy field.

Then he examined her, pointing at different parts of her body until the pendulum rotated to the left, thus indicating the problem. Thereafter he went to his cupboard to fetch a small tube of ointment. This he tested against her body, until the pendulum circled clockwise in approval.

"Rub this on your face in the morning and again last thing at night."

UNCLE JOSEPH DROPS A WORD

Within three days the ugly spots had gone.

"And what *was* in that little tube, Uncle?" I asked on hearing this tale.

"Plain English Medicated Vaseline," he replied with an ingenuous smile.

One day, long after Uncle Joseph had retired, and settled in the south of France, he met a man who told him he was about to travel to Cairo.

Uncle said, "I know the climate well, for I spent fifty years in Egypt. Don't rush around as soon as you get there. The organism needs time to get acclimatized. Just relax and rest for the first three days."

The man took this advice to heart, and called on Uncle Joseph on his return.

"Monsieur," he said, "I did as you suggested. The other members of the group rushed around sightseeing from the first instant, but I remembered your advice. So I stayed behind and gave myself time to adapt."

He chuckled.

"When they saw me resting in my deckchair they laughed at me for "wasting my time." However, by the middle of the week all of them were sick, except me."

UNCLE JOSEPH DROPS A WORD

Uncle's research also extended to architecture. When he lived in Egypt he even hired a young architect (who later became famous) to restructure his house so as to incorporate an arch.

"The arch breaks down the rays," Uncle said. "Depending on where you position yourself beneath it, you will receive a specific energy."

Knowing this once enabled him to help a man who suffered from an incurable condition. Aunty and Uncle often entertained a large number of guests in Cairo, for Uncle never accepted invitations to dine at other people's homes and always invited everyone to his.

One day one of the guests brought along a man who had had terrible headaches ever since he had served as a soldier in the First World War. He had consulted many doctors, but none had been able to cure him. That evening his head hurt particularly badly.

So his friend went to Uncle Joseph.

"Is there anything you can do to help him?"

"There is one thing I can try," he replied.

Uncle led the soldier to the arch in the living-room, took out his pendulum, asked him to hold out his left palm to obtain his

UNCLE JOSEPH DROPS A WORD

note, positioned him at one end of the arch and said, "Now inch your way forward."

He observed the rotation of the pendulum till he had identified the exact spot under the arch that would counteract the trouble and restore balance.

"Stop, and stand here for ten minutes."

Leaving the soldier there to absorb the corrective ray, Uncle Joseph returned to his guests. When ten minutes had elapsed, he fetched the soldier, took him to the guest room and said,

"Now lie down for half an hour."

When the ex-soldier returned, his terrible headache was gone, never to return.

To escape from the summer heat, Aunty and Uncle would move to Switzerland and spend July and August in Gstaad.

One day, many years later, a stranger walked up to them at their hotel.

"Hallo," she said, with a broad smile. "I am so glad to bump into you again."

Uncle Joseph could not place her.

"I'm sorry," he said, "I cannot recall your name."

UNCLE JOSEPH DROPS A WORD

The woman who stood before him burst out laughing.

"You do not recognize me?" she teased.

But no, she did not resemble anyone they had ever met before!

"I am so happy to meet you again after so many years! For you see, *I* am the hopeless case you once met at the spa in Brittany. *I* am that miserable, overweight woman with innumerable ailments and countless complaints!"

Aunty and Uncle looked stunned.

The woman smiled with evident pleasure.

"Desperate, I followed your advice to the letter! I ate slowly, just as you had suggested, and told myself a joke between every mouthful. At first it felt like a circus routine: take-a-bite, fork-down, chew-chew-chew, think-joke, swallow!"

She looked at him with a smile.

"But after a while I even began to enjoy myself. Before long I began to feel better. One by one my ailments diminished, and by the end of the year I was completely cured."

Uncle Joseph studied her. The slender woman standing before them was vibrant with health.

"And here am I, just loving life!"

UNCLE JOSEPH DROPS A WORD

Impulsively, she took Uncle's hand in hers, and looked into his eyes.

"*Monsieur,* I cannot thank you enough."

Uncle Joseph's Keys

Uncle Joseph is a prominent citizen. Part of the environment has been remodeled according to his advice. But he does not claim to be highly educated or particularly wise; nor indeed that he is *Somebody*. He could be a Buddhist, Theosophist, Sufi, Christian or simply a Businessman. It is hard to tell, for the business he minds is his own. He never sets himself up as a teacher, nor does he impose his beliefs.

I had thought Uncle would want to teach

me, but he made no move to do so. All I got to hear was: *I have nothing to sell!* This didn't make any sense to me and only left me nonplussed. Then he would add, so matter-of-fact, *Ask and you shall receive.* It felt so dry. But Uncle was against anything that tended to imprison, either himself or others.

"Don't be afraid of losing your way," he said one day "You will find new signposts to guide you."

I remember how a young man had asked him, "What is the purpose of life?"

And Uncle Joseph's startling reply:

"To place one foot ahead of the other!"

But now he continued: "If someone approaches you, shake hands; if he wants to follow you, share; if he wants to leave, let him go. Let no one impose an obligation on you. That's freedom. And if someone asks nothing of you, then give nothing."

But whenever I ask a serious question, Uncle Joseph breathes counsel like a gentle wind.

"I am the prompter," he says. "Nothing more."

With exquisite courtesy Uncle Joseph inspires or suggests. One morning, as we wind our way up a quiet street lined with Cypress trees, some a hundred and fifty years old, I

UNCLE JOSEPH'S KEYS

have a burning question.

"What is Truth? *Exactly!*"

"Child," he says, "there is only one Source. Truth is always simple. There are many paths to Truth, but only one Fountain."

"But how can I find it?"

"Look for it in your own heart."

Uncle meets my incredulous gaze.

"I will give you a simple formula that will set you free," he says with an innocent smile, "THIH."

I stare at him in amazement.

Unperturbed, Uncle continues:

"Whenever you hear someone teach, be it the highest authority, the most impressive guru, the greatest scientist or the most famous professor, listen respectfully. Then say to yourself, *Thus have I heard*. Go into the quiet of your own heart, and ask yourself, *Is this true for me?* Listen in carefully. If the answer is *Yes*, then cherish it. But if it is *No*, then this is not for you.

"Trust your heart. It will unfailingly reveal the right answer. Each time you discover something that is true for you, you will have another block with which to build your inner Temple."

UNCLE JOSEPH'S KEYS

Uncle Joseph lived in the here and now and wasted no time on the past. However, the past worried *me*.

"Uncle," I said one day, "if I had known all this, I would have done things differently."

Uncle looked at me kindly, he who never judged.

"Life is like climbing a mountain. When you stand at its foot and look around, you base your actions on what you can perceive. As you ascend, the perspective broadens; you see more clearly. Halfway up you can see further; you discover that the vista little resembles what you saw when you first set out. But at the peak your horizon has become wider than anything you ever imagined. You can see a great distance. And once again, you may find yourself wishing: *Oh, if only I had known, I would have acted differently*. Regrets are a waste of time.

"Do not judge yourself. The fact is, you did *not* know. The person you were then could not have acted differently. It is only when one becomes aware of the right thing to do and disregards it, that one may blame oneself."

Uncle continued gently. "But remember, even at the peak, there is always more. And so it is also with Truth."

His words felt like balm to the soul. Guilt,

UNCLE JOSEPH'S KEYS

laid on me from tender youth, began to dissolve. Uncle smiled at me.

"Just do your best every day," he said, "and enjoy the present!"

Aunty and I had been writing letters in the dining room. It was a warm pleasant day and the window was open to an azure sky.

"Joseph has plenty of stamps," Aunty said, as I slipped my letter into the envelope.

When I knocked on the door of Uncle's study he was engrossed in his work. A stack of papers lay on his desk, beside the usual glass of water that he sipped throughout the morning. His face was flushed, as it always was when concentrating intensely for a long while. He looked up.

"Have you got a stamp for me, Uncle?"

Uncle Joseph put his pen down.

"This is the *third* time this week you have come in here for a stamp!"

Gracious! Uncle had always been Patience itself!

"The first thing I learnt was never to neglect the foundations," he said. "This can also be applied to everyday things. Like right now! You could just as easily go to the Post Office yourself and buy the stamps you'll need for a month!"

He reached for his flat leather stamp case.

"When undertaking anything, be it something simple or a spiritual quest, always lay a solid foundation. Some day you may feel the need to go back to those very beginnings."

All this! And just for a stamp!

"Let me tell you a story," he said, seeing my disarray. "I have studied graphology; and so has my middle brother. One can tell so much from a person's handwriting. Now a few years ago my hand was no longer steady, and my writing began to resemble a scrawl. So when my brother received my letter he showed it to his wife: 'Look at this letter; Joseph's handwriting has deteriorated! He is obviously not well!'"

An enchanting smile spread across Uncle's face. "I had no intention of letting such notions circulate. First they say one is not well, the next thing that one is sick; and soon one is at death's door! I did not need thoughts of this kind around me. So I bought a child's exercise book, a bottle of ink, and an old-fashioned pen with a nib, and went back to the foundations of learning to write. Every day I practiced forming large letters and words between two lines, as might a child at school. I did this until my hand had regained control and one day my handwriting was back to normal. So next time I wrote to my brother, he took the letter to his wife, and said, 'Look, Joseph must be well again. His writing is as beautiful as it was before'"

Uncle smiled with evident delight. "But, you see," he said, "there is a Spanish proverb: *Only the lid knows what is in the pot.*"

We are going on an outing. Aunty is at the wheel. She brakes sharply and toots vigorously (whether or not another car is in sight) as she prepares to drive the old black Peugeot through another tunnel on the "Middle Corniche". This is *her* way of accosting the Invisible.

Uncle makes no comment about his wife's driving - now, or ever.

We arrive at last. We are at *La Colline,* the Hill; it is covered with wild Rosemary, Sage and Thyme. The air is fresh; the hill looks inviting. Uncle puts his grey and white checked woolen shawl around his shoulders. He leans on his walking stick on the uneven path. His black boots gather dust.

The hairpin bends have left me feeling carsick. I ask Uncle if he can help me.

UNCLE JOSEPH'S KEYS

He takes his pendulum out of the small, square navy blue bag in which he always carries it, and prepares to identify my personal frequency. His left hand points lightly at my solar plexus, as he watches the movement of his instrument. He adjusts the string along the copper arch that he moves to the appropriate angle, and holds it at the second knot, most sensitive to biological energy fields. Next, he tests the plants growing around us, till the pendulum indicates the remedy.

Uncle stoops to break off a sprig of thyme and holds it close to my body. The pendulum circles at increasing speed. Satisfied, he hands me the thyme.

"Put this on your chest, and tell me when it becomes uncomfortable."

Its living energy enters my body like a soothing balm. I begin to feel better.

"You see," he says, "this plant was growing here silently, just being, and I picked it. It gave itself willingly, according to the Eternal Law: one thing must die, that another might live."

I listen, not very willingly.

But Uncle does not let go.

"Suffering is inevitable," he continues. "Every cell must die, to make room for another. *That* is the whole secret of life."

UNCLE JOSEPH'S KEYS

"It's starting to itch now, Uncle."

"Remove it."

I extract the sprig of thyme.

"Look at it," he insists.

I do; it has wilted.

"It gave you its life."

I feel guilty.

Uncle continues earnestly: "Live like this plant. Give, give, and give again - give until you can give no more, and then - give yet more."

But Uncle Joseph is no peddler of sorrows. He believes that all suffering holds a hidden blessing. One day, in a dark mood, I challenge him in the ancient, creaking lift!

"You often repeat that *behind every appearance of calamity there is good*! Just tell me, what *good* could you possibly invent for your accident?"

The mere thought of that reckless rider who knocked him down, fills me with rage. Uncle is pensive.

"Well! What good did you manage to find in *that*?" I repeat belligerently.

When at last Uncle speaks, he does so with unshakeable peace.

"There was great good in it," he says. "Before the accident I thought I had to attend every meeting, be at every lecture, read every

UNCLE JOSEPH'S KEYS

newspaper and magazine. I felt I had to be up-to-date on everything."

"What's so wrong with *that*?"

"But suddenly all this came to an end, and I found that life went on perfectly well without me. The accident taught me that no one is indispensable, and most certainly not I. In fact, it showed me how unimportant I really am."

Uncle Joseph's eyes rest on me serenely.

"And *that* gave me new freedom!"

One Easter vacation, I told Uncle that my father had given me three rules for living: "Always do your best; never be base, and always obey the dictates of your conscience, and by this I mean *your own* conscience, and *not* someone else's."

And so in turn I asked him:

"Do *you* have any life rules to share with me?"

And that was how, with a twinkle in the eye, Uncle Joseph delivered his ultimate key:

"Read the Bible, and keep your bowels clean!"

UNCLE JOSEPH'S KEYS

Some days later I developed another burning question.

"Uncle, the Heart is made for love. Why, then, does marriage so often not work?"

I really needed to know.

The Old Man looked at the Little Girl pensively and exclaimed, "It's all a matter of electromagnetic energy!"

I stood there, rooted to the spot. This was far worse than anything he had said so far. What I wanted was reassurance, not declarations about electromagnetic energy! At least he could have said something encouraging!

"You see," he continued, unperturbed, "at the beginning, when two people fall in love, the attraction is powerful, both organisms need each other and there is an interchange of magnetism beneficial to both. The trouble begins when one of the partners begins to get saturated. Irritation sets in and quarrels follow shortly after. The cause of the discord is often insignificant: saturation is what it is all about."

"There must be something one can do?"

"There is. The key lies in moderation. Never abuse the body, then it will serve you to a ripe old age."

UNCLE JOSEPH'S KEYS

Uncle read my disbelief.

"There are many ways of being married," he continued. "Some people are extremely independent and still have a successful marriage. The best example I ever saw was that of two remarkable people who later became our friends. Madame agreed to marry Monsieur *on condition that he agreed* for her to go on living in her own house! So he bought the house on the other side of the road, directly opposite hers, and there they were: a happy couple for life."

None of this sounded like love to me.

"You see," I wrote to my girlhood friend in utter dismay, "there is no such thing as love after all."

When her reply came back from Australia, the letter held a key.

"You are perfectly right!" she replied. "Love begins as an illusion; but the great challenge is to *recall* that illusion, and to *turn* it into reality. We are free to hand-make our happiness like that, day by day."

Uncle Joseph had married in his late fifties, and was to remain married for thirty-five years. One day he talked about love again.

"The nearest one can get to a definition of Love," he said, "is the Italian, *Ti voglio bene*. The words literally mean *I wish you well*."

UNCLE JOSEPH'S KEYS

"Why did you marry Aunty?"

Uncle smiled tenderly, enigmatically.

"She was a flower!"

That was all he said that day.

But a few days later, on our morning walk, the subject came up again. Aunty was displeased with me — yet again. Uncle had witnessed the scene and was obviously affected. We had left the flat in a somber mood.

"You and Aunty are so different," I said to him at last. "How did you manage to stay with her for so long?"

"I could not have done so if I had not studied astrology. She has a very difficult chart and that enabled me to understand her better. Thereafter it became a little easier."

At last, he was telling me more!

"Child, if you want to evolve, marry someone as different to you as possible."

On another occasion I was privileged to witness an amazing expression of Love.

Uncle was in high spirits, and began to talk about marriage again.

"I made a terrible faux-pas once," he began. "Some friends invited me to a wedding, and so I attended. After the ceremony the groom stood outside to receive the well wishes of friends. One by one the

UNCLE JOSEPH'S KEYS

guests shook his hand, and congratulated him.

"Mes félicitations," they said, one after the other.

When my turn came I shook the groom's hand and smiled at him like the others; like the others I stepped forward to congratulate him - but what actually slipped out was *"Mes condoléances."*

Then I walked away absentmindedly. I was half way home before I realized what I had done!

Aunty laughed. "But we have done much worse than that," she added. "One day we had some special visitors. They were an unhappy couple, and the husband confided in us that he was considering divorce.

"We wanted to show them a mark of affection and to cheer them up. So we thought it would be a good idea to take them out to the theatre. Now, neither your Uncle nor I knew much about theatre, for we virtually never go to plays. So we chose one that sounded good, and bought tickets for the best seats.

"But it was a dreadful mistake. To our unutterable shame, the whole play turned out to be about a couple in the throes of divorce."

UNCLE JOSEPH'S KEYS

They had a good laugh as they recalled the event.

One Friday evening during the Easter vacation, the subject of marriage came up again.

"Marriage is for emphasizing how alone one is," Aunty began at dinner one night. Uncle listened quietly. Now, Aunty played the piano, loved classical music, and appreciated concerts given by the best conductors. As her husband was not particularly interested, she always went to these concerts alone. She greatly looked forward to such evenings. For her it was also an escape from domesticity.

"There's something I have never told you," Aunty continued.

"Many years ago, a famous conductor came to our town. I went to his concert and sat in the front row. It was out of this world. I was deeply moved. So I went up afterwards, took hold of his hand, looked into his eyes, and thanked him from the bottom of my heart. I could not help myself," she added, suddenly radiant.

Aunty paused as she looked back into the past.

"The truth is, I had fallen in love with him."

UNCLE JOSEPH'S KEYS

Uncle looked at her tenderly.
"You should have told me, my dear, and I would have left you free."

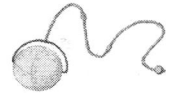

Uncle Joseph Breathes into Clay

Uncle Joseph did not set himself up as a judge; no, he was the humblest of men. Sixty-two years separated his wisdom from my sore lack of it. Contact with him was simple and direct. Not a relative by blood, this was an Uncle by soul. I was drawn to him as a sunflower towards the sun.

In our family we were all very *different*.

My father liked to talk about mountains and machines; he preached about education, health and exercise; he was passionate about the intelligence of wild animals.

My mother talked about God, the Church, the Priest, and was passionate about the Pope; she preached about religion, and complained about the maid. My mother maneuvered and told stories, mostly about witches.

My father engineered and told facts, such as: "Did you know that the incredible skulls in the Anthropology Museum (nothing more than upgraded monkeys, orangutans and apes) were actually those of our *ancestors*?"

He'd seen them. Face to face!

From this union issued three daughters, likewise different and unique: two close

UNCLE JOSEPH BREATHES INTO CLAY

together at the top, and nine years later, *The Child*, at the end.

When we were grown, we three sisters would often visit our Aunt and Uncle on the French Riviera. We'd fly in from different continents, one at a time, but when more than one of us arrived, a simple visit could turn into quite a happening. Then our different shades of uniqueness (each a goddess in her own right) would confront solidarity. Added to Aunty (the presiding deity) and the maid (the grumbler-in-chief) our ages spanned over half a century.

On such occasions Uncle Joseph, calm and composed, would sit through meals maintaining a kind of benign neutrality. But he needed all the virtue he could muster. It was then that, in the privacy of his study - his *Nursery*, as he sometimes called it — he would resort to his faithful tools: both *Patience* and *Keep Smiling* would then appear on his mantelshelf, where they could not fail to catch his eye.

Aunty (my father's sister) considered it her moral duty to hone one's character (if one had any, that is) and any member of the family was rightful material for her to work

UNCLE JOSEPH BREATHES INTO CLAY

on. So when all these unique women, together with the grouchy maid, began to foment disorder in the space of the small apartment, it would have taken a saint to put up with the result.

Uncle Joseph was that saint! He seemed to hear nothing, see nothing, and find nothing to say, and nearly always managed to keep smiling. The Elder's presence was a haven of peace.

Differences between the older and the younger, the respectable and the less so, could be aired vociferously - mostly at dinner. And if *The Child* refused to toe the line, the result was sure to be dramatic. Then Aunty would intervene, tut-tut (with fervent interpellations to *her* children) and call us all to order.

At such times the Elder could not help hearing everything, seeing everything; yet he found nothing to contradict and nothing to say. Until the day he drew the line; then addressing us in a voice of thunder, he cut sharp and clean.

"You are three young ladies with completely different natures, born into the same family. Each of you is made to command - but *not* one another!"

UNCLE JOSEPH BREATHES INTO CLAY

Next day I asked Uncle:

"What is one supposed to do when life gets *like this*?"

"Child, you react too quickly! Be alert and watch. When faced with an event that bothers you, say to yourself: *Tiens, c'est nouveau! Voyons qu'est-ce que c'est!* Look, this is new! Let's see what it is! Use this little formula the moment something disturbs you; before you label it good or bad. It will create an interval, intrigue your mind, and make it stop to observe."

One could trust Uncle; he spoke from experience.

"Caught in the heat of the moment, repeat: 'Look, this is new! Let's see what it is!' In this way you will find it easier to keep calm."

Uncle did his best to sow in me some seeds of wisdom, but I did not make a good pupil. So, unbeknown to me, he conferred with his spiritual adviser: what to do about the Young One?

They decided that some form of encouragement was called for.

"Aymone wants to give you a gift," Uncle told me. "But you will have to be patient,

UNCLE JOSEPH BREATHES INTO CLAY

while we think about it."

I was so excited!

Here I was, being initiated into matters mysterious, such as stars that influenced one's life, colors that translated into musical notes, and essential oils whose frequency corresponded to colors, tones and gemstones. I must be due for a special ring, I thought; after all, both Uncle and Aymone had one. I anticipated the great moment. A ruby would be just right! For energy!

On a cold March day, Aymone came to visit me in London and handed me a knobbly package. I fingered it, felt it, and opened it: out came a bronze figurine of three little monkeys. The first covered his mouth with his hands, the second his eyes and the third, his ears.

"This is a talisman," she said gently. "The three little monkeys invite you to develop the right attitudes to life and will encourage you to surpass yourself."

But I looked at them in dismay.

Oh, No! Not my ancestors again!

UNCLE JOSEPH BREATHES INTO CLAY

"The Three Wise Monkeys are a symbol of the perfection to strive for, and teach one to See No Evil, Hear No Evil and Speak No Evil. As long as our senses are not rooted in a spiritual tradition, sight, hearing and speech cannot be trusted. Like the Three Monkeys we must See Everything, Hear Everything and Say Nothing," she continued.

That gave me plenty to think about.

"This teaching also contains its opposite: See Nothing, Hear Nothing, Find Nothing to Contradict and Nothing to Say."

This sounded to me like Uncle's way!

"These two formulae can prevent one from making mistakes. But one needs to pay attention and apply discernment. The Three Wise Monkeys demonstrate how this can be done."

I put the figurine on the mantelpiece in my bedroom and would look at it askance from time to time. But all it ever did for me was to

UNCLE JOSEPH BREATHES INTO CLAY

remind me of the Vervet monkeys that invade dwellings in South Africa to steal food. And with that, I lost all interest in further spiritual lessons!

Aymone was troubled and confided in Uncle. The following summer Uncle had a simple ring made for me - of silver, copper and gold.

"Wear it on your little finger," he said. "It will balance your energy."

And his smile fell like balm upon my heart.

I wore the ring for years, as proudly as a Queen, until the day it mysteriously disappeared.

As for encouragement, there was still a great deal for me to learn. Every year, one of my greatest joys was to look for a birthday card for my Uncle. So I would hunt around until I thought I had found the right one. In response, he would always write me a beautiful letter.

For his eighty-second birthday, I sent Uncle a card on the front of which was a painting of a magnificent old oak. It was with great joy that I received a long letter from him not long after.

Below is a translation of Uncle's reply to

UNCLE JOSEPH BREATHES INTO CLAY

the girl I then was:

It is my pleasure to come to have a little chat with you this morning. We have had visitors from Egypt, Switzerland and Kenya; have had to deal with business matters and with all that has taken place since we left Cairo in 1948. Almost three weeks have passed without leaving us time for correspondence; this is the reason for my delay in coming to say "How do you do" and to thank you for your birthday greetings on the occasion of my entry into the eighty-third cycle of my physical existence on earth, and to congratulate you on the poetical way you expressed them.

Your birthday card really charmed us, your Aunt as well as your Uncle, because it is infused with a cheerful, youthful philosophy that inspires one and does one good; especially as it emanates from a being such as yourself who feels and conceives deeply. This is wonderful for your age; may God help you develop this quality of the soul that makes life joyful and helps it to blossom naturally, with the fewest complexes.

Many years ago I came across a little book, called "Flowers and Gardens," which develops the image of human beings as flowers in the

UNCLE JOSEPH BREATHES INTO CLAY

Garden of the Creator. Your letter and the symbolic oak tree you chose to represent me, draws me back into the past, into an existence of work and idealism, studies and experiences, research and "discoveries." These make me feel that we live in a wonderful world and fill me with admiration and reverence for the Creator, and with joy in the increasing awareness of the workings of His Creation and of the Flowers in His Grandiose Garden.

I am not able to know and appreciate them all, but for me, those that Life put on my path bear witness to the Grandiose Wisdom of the Supreme Gardener who placed together the Rose and thorns, and gave the Hawthorn the inestimable virtue of balancing the rhythm of the heart, that is sometimes excited beyond right measure by the perfume of the Rose. The thorn of the Hawthorn has a sharper sting than that of the Rose, but that does not stop it from being beneficial. It is precisely in this that there is a lesson for us to learn: namely, that in all suffering; in every sting in Life – there are teachings – which, if well-used, help us re-establish our physical, emotional, mental and spiritual equilibrium, every time it is disturbed by the external world and our own make up. These, my dear, are the thoughts that arose this

UNCLE JOSEPH BREATHES INTO CLAY

morning on reading your delightful birthday greetings.

I spent a peaceful birthday; we only had the visit of one member of the family; my nephew came from London. Aunty decorated the table and a chocolate cake, topped by eight white and two rose candles, lighted in broad daylight, completed the ceremony. I must tell you that I was not as clever as you, and I was not able to blow out all ten candles with the same breath as you did when we celebrated your eleventh birthday at our hotel in Cape Town, the memory of which now returns. (....)

Here, after some sunny days, the cold weather is back; it is raining and we had to light the stove again. In spite of this, one can feel that spring is not far away. I hope that your end of winter is pleasant and that you are enjoying life while at the same time working and preparing a pleasant future.

With much love,
Uncle Joseph

When Uncle turned eighty-four, I sent him a card depicting a carefree barefooted lad astride a donkey, dangling in front of the creature's mouth a long stick extended by a

UNCLE JOSEPH BREATHES INTO CLAY

string, to the end of which is tied a carrot - just out of reach. Eagerly the donkey trots towards it.

That year the Elder made it quite clear that he, too, needed encouragement. "I loved your birthday card," he wrote back. It makes a lovely gift. Please send me another ten!"

On my next visit Uncle Joseph said, "Your card was just right for me. You see, I need a carrot too. For *I* am the donkey."

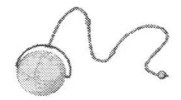

UNCLE JOSEPH OBEYS HIS DOCTOR

Uncle Joseph's brothers lived far away and enjoyed coming to visit him. Whenever they came Uncle changed. Within the bond of his family and all the memories it held for them, he looked somehow fuller and stronger.

He presided at the head of the table; he was their undisputed chief. Animated conversation and pleasure rippled around the dining-room. The members of his *clan* would

UNCLE JOSEPH OBEYS HIS DOCTOR

come with their wives. Aunty would prepare five-star midday meals for them and act as their chauffeur, shuttling them to and fro from their hotel. She always made a point of being very polite to her husband's family. During these visits Uncle tended to become somewhat remote with me and I simply kept quiet.

One April it was his youngest brother, Schmol, who arrived with his wife, Jerusha. Schmol had recently retired; free time weighed heavy on his shoulders, and he had become restless. Everything got on his nerves.

His wife decided he needed a break; a holiday near his brother on the French Riviera would do him good. So she wrote to Uncle Joseph. She thought it would be nice to be near them.

Uncle rented for them the furnished apartment next door to theirs on the left, temporarily available while the owners were away. Then he wrote to say that he invited them to stay for one month.

The next letter from Jerusha announced that they would be coming for six! Indeed, they arrived with enough luggage for a whole year.

One day Schmol ran a bath while his wife was out shopping. Then he forgot all about it,

UNCLE JOSEPH OBEYS HIS DOCTOR

and went off to post a letter. By the time he got back the bath had overflowed, its water swirled on the floor and had begun to leak through the ceiling into the flat below. When Jerusha returned and saw what had happened, she chided her husband – severely.

The owners of the apartment directly beneath them were away, so no one was able to enter to assess the damage - *if any*, of course.

When they returned, they were appalled at what they found. Leaving an indecent smudge in the middle of the ceiling, the water had trickled down onto the duck-egg blue wallpaper and onto a set of chairs upholstered in matching brocaded silk. Mould had set in. A precious painting had been spared, but the water had soaked into the Persian carpet. The entire room had to be redecorated.

However, matching material to reupholster the chairs could no longer be found, and for the same reason none of the wallpaper could be saved.

They presented Schmol with a heavy bill for damages. Jerusha was enraged. This went far beyond what she could bear.

UNCLE JOSEPH OBEYS HIS DOCTOR

So much money! Such stupidity!
And who was going to pay for all this?

Then she stopped wringing her hands and set to with determination. She told off Schmol day after day, till Schmol could stand it no more. He threatened to jump out of the window and frequently repeated this, with theatrical, life-sized gestures.

Jerusha bestowed her full attention on the matter. Indeed, she could think of nothing else. Then she hit upon an ingenious plan; she would militate for her *rights*. Just because it was her husband who had done it, was absolutely no reason why *they* should have to pay! Joseph, her brother-in-law, was the eldest, and he was rich enough to deal with all this. He had invited them; it was he who had rented the apartment for them. Therefore it was – quite obviously – Joseph who should foot the bill!

Carried away by the sheer brilliance of her plan, Jerusha gave Schmol some reprieve and took on Uncle Joseph, setting on him with incomparable effrontery.

"*You* rented this flat for us, and this flat is in *your* building! So *you* are responsible, and *you* should be the one to pay."

Or I'll find a way to make you!

UNCLE JOSEPH OBEYS HIS DOCTOR

Day by day, hour by hour, Jerusha's voice grated on them as she gained momentum. Aunty cast her eyes up, and also the palms of her hands heavenwards: *and the expense*! Uncle Joseph began to look weary, but he was not impressed.

Schmol went on threatening to jump out of the window, and Jerusha continued to work on her brother-in-law. But the more she pestered, the deeper he retreated within. Undeterred, Jerusha maneuvered on.

"Really Joseph," she said, looking pained, "it's not my fault that my husband's bath leaked through the ceiling onto the silly old, moth-eaten carpet in the flat below. It's ridiculous to imagine that we should have to foot the entire bill! *You* should *at least* pay for part of the damage."

Aunty wrung her hands and walked the floor.

Uncle Joseph went *bone-pale*; but armed himself with *Patience*. Jerusha tackled him once, she tackled him twice; she tackled him thrice. She rang their doorbell relentlessly, determined to capture him. And still he held his peace; but he did show signs of wear.

This was certainly not the *first* time Uncle Joseph had been faced with a *Situation*. He had practiced patience, and he had tried to

UNCLE JOSEPH OBEYS HIS DOCTOR

keep smiling! He had sought the Essential and had dared to act upon it. He knew that even The Absurd could be essential. But *this* beat anything he had ever been through before.

Finally Uncle Joseph's patience ran out. Relying on sleep to bring clarity, he withdrew for the night.

The next morning he summoned the long trusted family doctor to come to see Schmol. Dr. Jacques was over eighty. Rooted in experience and steeped in wisdom, one could rely on him.

The doorbell rang. Aunty glued an eye to the peep-hole and breathed a sigh of relief. It was the family doctor with his black leather bag. Tall and frail, he had seen much of life.

He listened in silence, until he had heard them out. No, he did not wish to see the *baby* brother! Impassively he took out his pad, scrawled a few words on it, tore off the page, and handed it to Uncle Joseph; after which, with a polite bow, he left.

In the dim light of the hall, Uncle and Aunty pored over the pivotal prescription:

"Pack your bags at once, and leave!"

Instantly they began to pack: within three hours the Elder and his spouse were gone.

UNCLE JOSEPH OBEYS HIS DOCTOR

Bereft of his audience, Schmol declared himself cured. Jerusha was left to pack her bags and take her Schmol and her bill home.

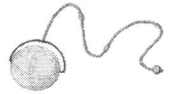

Uncle Joseph Lets Himself Be Tempted

Every Sunday Aunty goes to the Church-on-the-Hill, alone. She is not particularly fond of this Church; but it is the nearest. And every Sunday - without fail - she comes back from Mass with a headache, and has to lie down.

We are out on our morning walk under an azure dome. Uncle Joseph is happy and carefree today; no one would guess his age. The caps of his black leather ankle boots shine as he puts one foot forward after the other. Enthusiastically I fall in with his slow, measured steps. We cross the boulevard and pass an abandoned ochre mansion inhabited by stray cats, fed by a bent old woman. The street is lined by tall, resin-scented cypress trees dotted with cones, and winds uphill. This is also the way to Aunty's Church.

The fresh fragrance of opening blossoms envelops us. It is springtime; delicate colors whisper their melody as we pass, as on the strings of a harp. The olive grove is in full bloom, its low trees decked in white.

When the Church comes into sight, Uncle turns to me with a mysterious smile.

"Do you want to know what it is that gives

UNCLE JOSEPH LETS HIMSELF BE TEMPTED

your Aunt her Sunday Mass headaches?"

"Yes! Of course I want to know!"

"Long ago," he begins, "a temple stood on this site. It was dedicated to a pagan goddess. The Church you now see was built on its ruins. The foundations are probably still impregnated with the original vibration, and thus the force field is that of two religions superimposed. It must be to this that your Aunt is sensitive."

"But why doesn't she go to a different Church?"

"Indeed, I have tried to persuade her to do so, but she won't. There are two other Churches nearby, but she would have to take the car. Your Aunt is fiercely independent and prefers to walk."

Suddenly a devious plan forms itself in me. Uncle *could* investigate, *if* he wanted to! He *could* find out what just happens here. I have seen his pendulum at work and have unlimited confidence in it. One can ask it any question and get a precise answer.

The bubbles mount, the cork pops!

"U-n-c-l-e," I begin, hoping to put him up to some proper no-good, "have you got your pendulum with you?"

UNCLE JOSEPH LETS HIMSELF BE TEMPTED

He has, of course! I know he has. He never goes anywhere without it.

"Why do you ask?"

"Well, I have an idea! You could go right *inside* the Church to investigate! Wouldn't it be exciting to discover the cause of Aunty's mystifying headaches?"

"*Petite diablesse!*" he shoots at me. "You little imp! The answer is No!"

Uncle has great respect for other people's reality; normally he will not intrude on it.

Giddy with spring, I urge: "Oh, go on! This is a marvelous opportunity!"

The mere possibility fills me with delight.

"But the *padre* here knows me!" he protests mildly, as the rogue idea begins to take root.

"What does that matter? Tourists wander in and out of the Church all the time, so we would not be noticed. Besides, the *padre* is probably not even in!"

To delve into the mystery of life, to fathom out its hidden realms; to search the secret and the sublime: therein lies Uncle's passion!

His voice betrays him; he is thrilled. His eyes dance with fun; even the golden rim of his spectacles develops a glint.

"All right, then!" he says. "But you *are* a real little rascal! And there's no getting away

UNCLE JOSEPH LETS HIMSELF BE TEMPTED

from it!"

A flush spreads across his youthful face. His passion for inquiry is ignited. We push aside the heavy wooden door and enter the centuries-old gloom. Uncle stops and takes off his hat. I look around quickly, six-eyed; but no, we are alone. The Church is empty; the moment is opportune.

"Come on now, Uncle!" I whisper. "Don't hang around at the back of the Church. We must go half-way up the nave at least!"

Treading softly, we move forward. My imagination is on fire. What will he detect?

Uncle Joseph's pendulum is a marvelous instrument that enables him to identify the energies emanating from a specific person, object or place.

What will it catch?

Uncle takes a quick, sharp look around: conditions are ideal. First, he will measure the unique frequency of the Church. (This is like taking its temperature).

"The altars of many Christian Churches in England have long been tested by dowsers and found to be almost invariably positive. But specific points of re-used sites can carry energies of various types or concentrations of charge at certain parts on the structure, such as buttresses. So I must locate the

UNCLE JOSEPH LETS HIMSELF BE TEMPTED

cornerstone, for it will hold the first force field, and therein will lie its secret."

Intrigued, but by no means certain that he actually approves of himself, or of what he is about to do, Uncle Joseph now turns to face North and adjusts his pendulum for this unusual investigation. With the sure gestures of an experienced practitioner, he shifts the movable arch to the proper markings on the wooden sphere and raises his forearm to a right angle. His right hand supple and completely still, he lets the instrument dangle and oscillate till it steadies. His free hand points outwards; it is the antenna. In an attitude of quiet neutrality, he focuses on the question to explore. The moment to test his hypothesis is at hand.

Stock-still, I watch.

What will he uncover? Did strange primeval rites take place here, deep under the ground? Is the ancient cornerstone alive? Will it speak?

With breath suspended, I wait till Uncle is ready to begin. His right wrist is supple, his hand poised, immobile; his fingers hold the string lightly at the third knot (the most effective for detecting earth emanations). He uses his left hand as a pointer.

UNCLE JOSEPH LETS HIMSELF BE TEMPTED

The pendulum is in neutral, suspended in mid-air, as we hover on the brink of discovery.

But...

At that very moment a vague shape stirs in the shadows at the far end; a figure approaches. A black robe swishes and leather shoes creak, as step by step, it moves towards us through the eerie gloom.

Quick as lightning, Uncle whips the pendulum into his pocket.

Obscurity shrouds the face until he emerges into view. It is the parish priest!

Anxiously I anticipate the question now surely in his mind:

And what might you be doing Sir, if I may ask?

"*Bonjour,* Monsieur!" says the *Padre,* recognizing the husband of one of his Faithful. "May I help you?"

"Good day, *mon Père,*" replies my Uncle. "Thank you, but my niece and I are just visiting. Well, we must be leaving. Good-bye, Father."

Thereupon Uncle turns and in the same unruffled rhythm I know so well, the same small, measured steps I love, leads the retreat

UNCLE JOSEPH LETS HIMSELF BE TEMPTED

back down the central nave. We push open the heavy door and step into the brilliant blaze. The puzzled *padre* sighs and lingers till we are gone. We cross the courtyard, head for the garden and stroll along the path to a bench.

Safely seated, Uncle Joseph says,

"You see! We shouldn't have done it."

Then he adds,

"The priest must have sensed something. He came out just in time to protect his territory!"

It takes us a while to recover! Orange and tangerine trees scent the air, and Uncle enfolds me with that wonderful smile that keeps him perpetually young.

But from then on Uncle Joseph would not go near that Church again.

And yet, how delightful to discover in him the bold young hero entering mysterious ground in quest of discovery!

UNCLE JOSEPH RESPONDS TO THE MOMENT

Uncle Joseph lived by his pendulum. Wherever he went, he carried it around with him in a small, square bag.

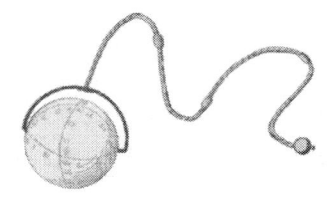

So much so, that once Aunty even said to me: "I can just see it coming! One of these days some old fogey is going to sidle up to me in the street and ask, 'Does your husband actually carry provisions on his walks?'"

Measuring *The Energies,* and adapting himself thereto, was what Uncle Joseph always did. All this was all very well if it took place in his home. But inevitably some need would send him into the theatre of the outside world.

He's not going to take his pendulum out here, in the Supermarket, is he?

UNCLE JOSEPH RESPONDS TO THE MOMENT

Living thus within his own order and harmony, Uncle Joseph maintained health, and reached a fine old age.

"One is not entirely bound by one's birth chart," Aymone told me one day. "In fact, one can jump its boundaries. That's what your Uncle did. He outlived his allocated span by about thirteen years. Astrological cycles are not a hundred per cent immutable. There is a window through which grace can enter. And if called upon, the action of grace can change everything."

Aligning himself with Cosmic Vibration was Uncle Joseph's life task, not that everyone around him thought this a particularly bright thing to do.

Uncle Joseph kept his feet firmly on the ground. He paid attention to that which had to be done each day, each hour, each moment. He noted for himself what he considered essential, and lived by it.

In one of Uncle's books we discovered a handwritten scrap of paper with these lines, which he had copied in French from a Buddhist book.

UNCLE JOSEPH RESPONDS TO THE MOMENT

Sow a thought, and you reap an act;
Sow an act, and you reap a habit;
Sow a habit, and you reap a character;
Sow a character, and you reap a destiny,
For character is destiny.

(Charles Reade)

Thus Uncle endeavored to establish only those habit patterns that renewed him, and to free himself of all that did not. All else came under relentless scrutiny.

Shaving was no exception.

In the tradition of the skilful gentleman shaver of previous centuries, Uncle Joseph owned a set of seven keen-edged, cut-throat razors of the finest Sheffield steel, with a smooth black handle. One for every day of the week.

Each had its own black cardboard box with a decorative grey label.

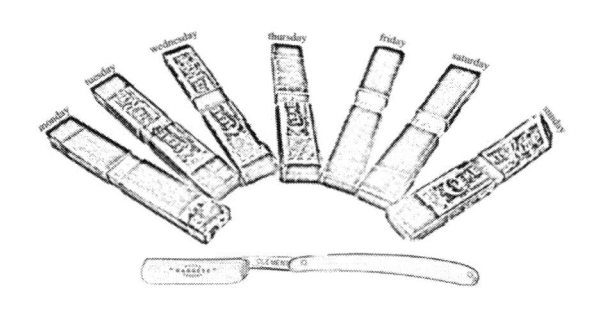

UNCLE JOSEPH RESPONDS TO THE MOMENT

Every morning Uncle gave himself such a skilful clean, close shave, that no one depositing a little kiss would ever have suspected that he needed to shave at all.

Thereafter he would clean the fine, sharp blade meticulously and put it back into its own box, ready for use again in seven days.

Each box bore the following offer in fine print:

Clements Razors
103, Strand,
London W.C.2
Under Savoy Hotel

When this Razor requires sharpening
please send it to the above address.

Resetting 9d
Ground and Set as new 1/6

Every morning Uncle had to find the day's box, but he maintained his practice with persistence, using Monday's razor only on a Monday, and Thursday's indeed only on a Thursday! For these boxes were not only individually marked with the days of the week, but each also bore its corresponding astrological sign: the moon for Monday, Mercury for Wednesday, Venus for Friday. And the Sun for Sunday. The only addition to

UNCLE JOSEPH RESPONDS TO THE MOMENT

this daily chore was the occasional honing of the razor's fine edge.

Uncle Joseph did not fight the stars; nor did he rail against them in adversity, but endeavored at all times to align himself to that which is. Was the radiation of the planets too electric, or too magnetic? Or not enough so? Or all of one thing, and none of the other? Uncle Joseph knew how to fix it! However, when it came to Uranus (especially when retrograde) he resigned himself to possess his soul in patience.

"It is my master," he said.

From time to time a situation would arise that could not be taken lightly. Thus it was that one summer in Switzerland, a newly married couple, relatives of a close friend, turned up to visit him at his hotel. It was a sunny day and they sat outside on the terrace. The wife, resplendent in white, was obviously expecting a child. The husband, considerably older than she, looked a little scraggy and his movements were somewhat jerky. One could see that being with Uncle Joseph did him a lot of good.

UNCLE JOSEPH RESPONDS TO THE MOMENT

Several other friends arrived, and an animated conversation took place. One of the party ordered large portions of ice-cream for everyone. Normally Uncle Joseph did not eat ice-cream, but now he found himself facing three scoops of vanilla with chocolate sauce, sprinkled with burnt almonds. But his attention was elsewhere.

"Look," he said, turning to me. "See that young woman in white? See how radiant she is! Life has gained the upper hand. Her husband is a concentration camp survivor."

As we began to enjoy our ice-cream, I noticed that Uncle did not touch his, and simply looked on in marvelous repose.

"Uncle," I urged, "it would be so nice if you could join us. Do ask your pendulum if you can have some. It might even say *yes*!"

"In that case," he replied, "the thing to do is to put my pendulum *away*!"

Which he then did. Whereupon he joined in and ate his ice-cream with the rest of us.

And everyone celebrated Life.

There were times, however, when Life could seriously challenge Uncle's disciplines and the daily acts he sowed.

UNCLE JOSEPH RESPONDS TO THE MOMENT

Take the time his study had to be redecorated. The old carpet was threadbare; the wallpaper had turned grey. Even he could not but agree; or at least, he could see no reason not to! After choosing the color scheme and wallpaper, there remained little else for him to do, but to remove his belongings – and himself.

Gone the established order of life!
Gone the comfort of certainty!
Gone the usual place for each thing, and the luxury of knowing where to find it again!
No instant colors or herbal teas!
No shelf for his faithful cards!
No easy access to his notebooks, or his leather case of stamps!
No bedside stand with its little pile of Holy Books: among these the Bhagavad-Gita, the Bible and his Noble Eightfold Path, leather-bound; nor safe place for his watch at night!

Only his set of cut-throat razors continued to house undisturbed in the bathroom, bearing the symbol of their celestial lineage: Mars for Tuesday; Jupiter for Thursday and Saturn for Saturday.

UNCLE JOSEPH RESPONDS TO THE MOMENT

(Ten years later Aunty passed them on to her nephew, who found them in perfect condition, and has treasured them ever since.)

Uncle was relegated to the attic that had once been the servant's, and now was used for storage. Set on a brick-red tiled floor, it was large and had a hand basin with running cold water. Its three steep wooden steps led to a sunny balcony that overlooked the street.

It was not a bad room. It was just *not his*.

Uncle had been doing his best to school himself out of fixed routines. One week he put his hairbrush in a different place every day; the next, his toothbrush. Needless to say, he did not always find them right away!

UNCLE JOSEPH RESPONDS TO THE MOMENT

So this was another opportunity! Uncle took with him only those stalwart guardians of his mind: the beige, green and blue cards. Not that they were going to be much help.

UNCLE JOSEPH RESPONDS TO THE MOMENT

The decorators were unable to begin work, or end it on the promised dates. So Uncle was stranded up in the attic with a stack of dusty suitcases and a rickety wrought-iron standing-lamp that had seen better days.

"But how did you manage?" I asked.

His eyes lit up with irrepressible gaiety.

"I pretended I was in an airplane," he said, with a delightful smile. "As long as it was up in the sky, I could have no other expectations. And That was That!"

UNCLE JOSEPH VISITS HIS PALACES

Walking with Uncle Joseph in the fragrant sunshine of the French Riviera, we slip out of time. Morning walks with him are moments of delight. But sometimes a walk with Uncle can turn into a happening.

His gentle smile reposes in humility. His eyes meet one in peace. His voice is serene. He does not claim to be very knowledgeable, nor particularly wise, but trusts the seeds of experience. In fact, he is a gardener. But the

UNCLE JOSEPH VISITS HIS PALACES

field he tends is his own life; the virtues he waters are patience and loving kindness. The pruning he does is on his own emotions. The perfume that pervades is that of wonder. Uncle Joseph lives in the rhythm of the seasons, and attunes himself to the Infinite.

A man of slight build, he carries himself erect. One could not think of him as old. Anchored in peace, there is peace within his walls. Of exquisite courtesy, he does not criticize or judge. Respectful of Tradition, he is yet a man infinitely new. But the law he obeys is not dictated from without. A man of few possessions, abundance is his.

It is half past ten. I hang around his closed door, waiting. Aunty gets hold of me:

"You are not to make your Uncle late - *again!* Back for lunch on time, *please!* Twelve o'clock, *sharp!* Got it?"

Being on time for lunch was an old bone of contention between Aunty and Uncle. The trouble had begun long ago in Cairo, where Uncle liked to disappear upstairs to his private sphere on the upper floor. Before going up he would leave instructions not to be disturbed. What he did up there Aunty never discovered. What she did know, however, was that once up there, Uncle would lose track of time.

UNCLE JOSEPH VISITS HIS PALACES

In those days Uncle Joseph's mother lived with them. When dinner was ready, Aunty would wait, ready to serve the meal. But Uncle did not always remember to come down. "We never knew whether we should begin lunch without him, or not," my Aunt once told me. "His mother would ask me, *What on earth is he doing up there?* But I was not able to tell her! One day your Uncle only came down at half past two!"

So whenever Uncle and I arrived back from our walk a little late for lunch, Aunty would get doubly upset; cross for now and cross for then! And sometimes, as today, she would be angry with me before we had even left the flat!

It is a quarter to eleven; it is rather late for a walk, but Uncle had some urgent work to complete. We emerge from the apartment, and walk up the tree-lined boulevard. Uncle slips his hand into mine. I love to feel his hand; it is a touchstone to bliss. However, just today he decides to take the longer route.

It is a brilliant, cloudless day in June. We walk under the azure sky, and pass several ochre villas with mint green shutters, till we find ourselves in front of a wisteria, whose

UNCLE JOSEPH VISITS HIS PALACES

gnarled stem winds its way up the front of a mellow mansion and cascades down in little bunches of lilac blossoms.

A rhapsodic expression on his face, Uncle stops to admire it. "This lilac is so beautiful," he says. "It is the color of the soul."

We cross the boulevard and head towards the scented public garden surrounded by a low, warm wall. Tended with beauty and grace, this is a place of quiet. We enter through the high black wrought iron gate and pass the old gardener, who straightens up and doffs his cap. He smiles indulgently as we head for the rose-covered pergola, for he knows Uncle Joseph well.

Roses tumble in profusion on its arches. They dot the horizon in clusters of pink, white, yellow and crimson, and scent the air. Some are in bud; others in full bloom. Some are beginning to wilt or are about to lose their petals.

Uncle is pensive as we stroll on till we reach a heavy stone bench and sit in comfortable silence. After a while he says, "Let us continue."

So we walk on a little. Suddenly he stops again, turns to me earnestly and asks:

"Do you see this view? See this garden? This wood? This hill?"

UNCLE JOSEPH VISITS HIS PALACES

His voice rises passionately as his arms spread out to encompass all that is around him.

"Do you see it?"

Of course I see it!

"Well," he declares, "all this is mine!"

We pause for a while, then stroll along the path under the pergola.

"These roses are magnificent!" he says, stopping to inhale their scent.

Uncle extracts his pendulum from its small, square navy blue bag and slips it into his pocket.

"Hold the bag open for me, please."

He takes out a tiny mother-of-pearl penknife and snips a spent bloom above the neck.

"Uncle! What? Here?? In a public garden???"

"*Young One!*" he retorts, unconquerable. "Tomorrow its petals will lie on the ground."

I stand there, rooted to the spot.

Undaunted, and as if we have all the time in the world, Uncle now reaches for another wilted rose and plucks it. Its petals crinkle like cigarette paper as they drop into the bag. Then he picks a yellow bloom, its petals about to fall.

Peaceful and unconcerned, he deadheads

the roses. A sprig here, a single rose there, and the bag begins to fill.

In the distance the castle cannon booms: the clock strikes twelve. It is *Midi*, the sacred hour. Offices and factories come to a standstill as people jump into their cars or leap onto their mopeds and, with a single purpose, honk their way through the congested streets back home for lunch. *Midi* is dedicated to the Stomach-god. As the cacophony of the hour rises in worship, we hit clock time. But Uncle Joseph is lost in the moment, completely beyond time. Gently he cradles a newly opened ivory bloom; lost in wonder, his gaze innocent as that of a child.

"Look at the perfection of this rose," he murmurs. "It is God's creation."

Something, I cannot think what, makes me profoundly uneasy. Then my heart sinks.

Aunty! Oh! Aunty!

We're in for a very hot moment!
But Uncle looks at me with an impish grin.
"Rose petals make a wonderful tea," he says. "*And,* they can even calm a rage!"

UNCLE JOSEPH VISITS HIS PALACES

Contained as we are in our fragrant bubble and oblivious of all else, we have not noticed a solitary stroller, nor do we see him approach. Hot in the head, and red in the face, he irrupts, breathing heavily. His corpulence captures us.

Quick as lightning, I whip the bag out of sight, and step back. My eyes plunge into Uncle's. The man wags his nose into Uncle's face and roars, "Hey *Monsieur!* Aren't you ashamed of yourself?"

Uncle's hands freeze in mid-air - just for an instant - then he doffs his hat.

"Good afternoon, Sir!" he says, with the utmost courtesy.

The gruff man grunts as he stands over us. Uncle wipes the blade of his penknife, as if nothing has happened, folds it peacefully, and slips it into his pocket. After which, without a single word, he leads me forward. We pass the old gardener, who smiles as we leave. He is well-acquainted with Uncle's ways and had long given him his blessing.

We leave through the high wrought iron gates and head for home. An ill-tempered cloud overshadows us. The indignant man, himself in the grip of the lunchtime ritual, has caught up. Now he marches past in a blaze of ire. A convulsive sound escapes Uncle's

UNCLE JOSEPH VISITS HIS PALACES

throat. I dare not look at him. We manage to hold it until the man is out of earshot; then we explode: peals of laughter rock us till tears stream down our cheeks. Suddenly Uncle stops dead and extracts his pocket watch. It is a quarter past twelve.

"Sapristi!" he exclaims. "We're late for lunch!"

We are not only late; we're going to be half-an-hour late! For there is no way that Uncle can walk any faster. When the man is out of sight, Uncle suddenly protests,

"Why shouldn't I snip some faded roses?"

Uncle Joseph never said to me, *Do as I do!* He simply lived his own freedom.

Forty years later I return to the French Riviera, retrace our walks and visit this scented garden once more. I head for the rose-covered pergola to inhale the familiar perfume. The gay blooms of yellow, red and white attract the eye. Savoring every moment, I slowly make my way to the last beds. Here the profusion of crimson roses exudes a wondrous fragrance.

The old gardener has retired, of course,

UNCLE JOSEPH VISITS HIS PALACES

but I tell the new one that I used to walk here with my Uncle, so long ago.

"These are still the original rose bushes," he says, pointing to the crimson-covered stems. "They are *Arioso, une variété ancienne* – a species of rosebush no longer on the market."

He lets me pick a spent bloom – discreetly, please - to take home.

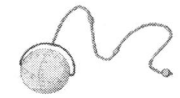

Uncle Joseph Dips into the Fountain

Uncle Joseph was not always the man he would one day become; the Uncle I met. It never occurred to me that he had not always been a sage; or to wonder how he had got to be that way. I was too young and ignorant to ask the questions I would ask today.

That morning he had said his *Morning Prayer* as usual, and had then settled to an hour of correspondence. His face still flushed from the effort of prolonged concentration, he said, "Come, let us post these letters, and go for a walk."

We set off up the boulevard. The sunbeams of the crisp winter's day drifted around us, and there was not a cloud in the sky. He began to relate some of the difficulties he had experienced in his life.

"I had to go to America once."

"What for?"

"The Director of my company sent me to open a branch, and I was to be there for some months. This gave me the opportunity to sort out a private problem. I had been having trouble with my back. The Americans had the most advanced Chiropractic techniques, so I enrolled in a College of Chiropractic, and moved into a flat-share with two others: one man and one woman."

"Uncle... *you?* In a mixed flat??"

"Oh, I thought nothing of it. We all had the same goal, and practiced on each other in the evenings. In fact, it would have been the perfect arrangement, had I been able to speak English properly. I had long taught myself to *read* English with the help of a dictionary, but that was a far cry from everyday speech. So I just kept quiet. One day, the other fellow, a tall American, said to me, "Joseph, what's the matter with you? You never say a word!"

"Taken aback, I said I did not know how to pronounce the words. "Just open your mouth and speak!" he retorted. So, once I had got over the shock, that's exactly what I did!"

Uncle laughed.

"America certainly is the place where one learns to let go of one's inhibitions."

Uncle was perfectly fluent in English. That he might once have had difficulties never occurred to me.

"I was shy, and this was a handicap for a long time. But around 1920 I met Emile Coué who discreetly took me in hand. He asked me to translate his book from French into English.

UNCLE JOSEPH DIPS INTO THE FOUNTAIN

"First, I read the book three times. Gradually, as I absorbed his ideas, I found myself repeating his mantra: *Every day, in every way, I am getting better and better.*"

"So you finished translating the book, and then what happened?"

"The next thing Mr. Coué wanted me to do was to give a lecture. In English! Well, I refused. I had no desire to stutter my way through it. What is more, I had a bandage around my head at the time, and did not wish to appear in public. However, he managed to persuade me. So in the end I gave the lecture."

"How did it go?"

Uncle chuckled. "Actually, it went well and did me a lot of good."

UNCLE JOSEPH DIPS INTO THE FOUNTAIN

Uncle had lent me this book and I read it. This sentence struck me: "It is not the years that make old age, but the belief that one is getting old; there are men who are young at eighty and others who are old at forty."

Uncle was such a man, who was young at eighty.

"But if you translated his book, Uncle, why is your name not in it?"

"I gave Mr. Coué the translation. It was *his* book. I did not need my name on it."

But for Uncle, more was still to come.

"You know," he continued, "I found that in America everything was so completely different to what I was used to. I could not help but marvel at the way the Americans did things. There was much that amazed me: houses that were put up in one day; meals that were prepared weeks in advance. These are marvelously efficient people and I love their pioneering spirit," he concluded.

We had reached a bench, and sat down. Uncle's expression softened and his eyes took on a faraway look.

"But it was in America that I experienced the real meaning of distance," he said.

I was fascinated.

UNCLE JOSEPH DIPS INTO THE FOUNTAIN

"One day, I had to take the train to a distant city. The journey seemed endless and I began to feel increasingly tired. Suddenly I realized I would have to interrupt my journey to rest. So I got out at the next station, and took a room at the railway hotel.

"As I prepared to lie down I noticed a Standard American Bible on the bedside table. The excellent index at the back of the book offered help for every ill.

> When things look blue, read Isaiah, Ch. 40
> If you are facing a crisis, read Psalm 46
> If you are sick or in pain, read Psalm 91

"I really appreciated the very practical American way of doing things! Then my eyes fell on one that felt just right for me:

> When you are very weary, seek Mat. 11:28
> Come unto me all ye that labor and are heavy laden, and I will give you rest. Take my yoke upon you and learn of me; for I am meek and lowly in heart; and ye shall find rest in your souls. For my yoke is easy, and my burden is light.

"As I read these lines aloud, the power of *His* words penetrated me. It was as if Jesus Christ was present in the room, speaking to me. Suddenly I felt refreshed and restored, filled with joy and strength, incredibly alive. My exhaustion vanished as if it had never existed. I found myself completely revitalized and had so much energy, that I could have taken the next train. And I thought I needn't have interrupted my journey at all."

It must have been there, in that hotel room, that Uncle Joseph had received the gift of that *Peace which passeth all understanding.*

Our walk is over. We are back in good time for a fresh hot meal. Aunty is happy and relaxed; she is going to the Opera that evening. Things have been running smoothly all day.

UNCLE JOSEPH'S TOOL BOX

Uncle Joseph has his own set of tools. His pendulum is his master tool. It deciphers the energies of the inner and outer environment, provides information and enables him to act upon it.

But for grooming the mind, heart and soul, he has three tools, three distinct cards that stand on the mantelshelf in his room, where they cannot fail to catch his eye.

The first of these is a card, four inches by three, on which is printed *Keep Smiling* in bold capitals on a blue background.

UNCLE JOSEPH'S TOOL BOX

Apart from its regular use as a daily reminder, this card once served a unique purpose.

In the course of his career, Uncle Joseph developed many skills. One day he was called in during a negotiation impasse; the protagonists were representatives of two major banks locked into an impossible conflict. Each party tried to outmaneuver the other. The men had been at loggerheads for three days. Finally they were obliged to seek the help of an experienced mediator.

Uncle Joseph listened to each party in turn. Then he asked the bankers:

"Do you really want to reach an agreement?"

"Of course!" they both assured him. "But we see no way out of the deadlock."

"Good!" said Joseph, smiling "Then this is the thing to do!"

Confident and relaxed, he took out his wallet, extracted a blue card and held it up for all to see the large letters.

Keep Smiling!

"To be fair," he continued, "both parties will get 50% of their demands, and both will have to give up 50%. So keep smiling!"

Caught by surprise, the protagonists could not help laughing, and soon reached an agreement. This only took a few minutes.

"And I was paid a fortune for my time," Uncle concluded.

That was not, however, the only occasion this card worked wonders.

"It was during World War I that I met a General who told me that his military people were getting depressed in the gloomy underground war offices. So I gave him a little pile of these cards, and suggested that he tack one to each door; which he did. From then on, as his men hurried down the long somber corridors, they would suddenly brighten up as they reached a door, and begin to smile. When the war came to an end, the General told me, 'Your *Keep Smiling* cards changed the whole atmosphere.'"

Uncle's second tool consists of just one word - *Patience* - printed in large capitals on a green background.

Uncle Joseph had not only developed great reserves of this virtue, (which as a family, we nonetheless at times nearly managed to exhaust) but continued to remind himself frequently to practice it.

Finally Uncle took it with him to eternity.

UNCLE JOSEPH'S TOOL BOX

As I stood again at the foot of his grave thirty years later, I actually *saw* it for the first time: chiseled into the granite tombstone is a single word: PATIENCE.

However, what Uncle actually felt about these silent companions — no doubt irksome at times - was something he never let on!

The third of Uncle's tools is his *Morning Prayer,* taken from "Poems of Power" by Ella Wheeler Wilcox, and printed on a card "by permission." It was to stand him in good stead.

One day Aymone phoned Uncle Joseph and asked to see him. A close friend of hers was asking for help, because her husband had got himself into trouble. To escape from moderate circumstances, Mr. Le Roy had betrayed his employer's trust, embezzled his money, bought himself smart clothes, joined the local Country Club and lived it up. The truth took time to come out. But when it did, his employer faced him with one alternative: immediate repayment in full, or jail.

Now Aymone stood awkwardly before Uncle Joseph. She had never asked him for anything before.

"Take a seat," he said with a smile.

UNCLE JOSEPH'S TOOL BOX

She sat down in the low, light blue armchair. "I have come to seek your help, *Monsieur*."

"What can I do for you?"

"My friend, Jeanine, asked me to speak to you on her behalf."

Aymone outlined the situation.

"I was wondering if you could possibly lend her husband the full sum of money he owes his employer? He promises to pay back every centime."

Uncle Joseph's smile vanished. Nothing like this had ever happened to him before. He had been intimately acquainted with adversity: he had been through poverty and deprivation, had lost his fortune three times; been close to death three times, and had to begin again. But integrity remained the value he prized most.

"In those days, a man's word was binding. It was a legal contract, and agreements were clinched by a handshake."

One day Uncle told me quietly, just in passing: "There was a certain man in Cairo, whose duty it was to visit the banks. Every morning he would set out on his rounds, calling in at one bank after the other. One day the Director of one of the banks said to him: Whenever you enter, the place is filled with

UNCLE JOSEPH'S TOOL BOX

light."

(It only dawned on me later that Uncle had been referring to himself).

Now, in Uncle Joseph's study, the silence was ominous. Aymone did not move; she dared not speak. She was well aware of his attitude to money. "Money is neither good, nor bad. It is an energy one must learn to work with."

Uncle never bought anything on credit. "Debt is a prison," he had so often said. But to be asked to lend money to a liar and a thief, and a considerable sum at that, came as a shock that landed on his chest like a dark, murky splodge.

Aymone stood before him, her heart thumping. She took a deep breath. At last her courage returned.

"I would be so grateful, *Monsieur*," she began, "if you could do this. Then Mrs. Le Roy will not be left destitute while her husband spends years in prison. She plans to take in sewing to help repay the loan."

So Uncle applied the timeless remedy: *La nuit porte conseil.* He would sleep on it.

"Phone me in the morning," he said, "and I shall give you my answer."

Hot and forlorn, Aymone left.

UNCLE JOSEPH'S TOOL BOX

Uncle Joseph faced his new day, no wiser than before. He had been unable to make up his mind and knew he would need all the virtue he could muster. Dolefully he placed *Keep Smiling,* out on his mantelshelf. Then he began his *Morning Prayer*.

> Let me to-day do something that shall take
> A little sadness from the world's vast store
> And may I be so favored as to make
> Of joy's too scanty sum a little more.

Uncle Joseph sighed; a deep sigh, straight from the heart. The shock that had landed on his chest, like a dark, murky splodge, lightened a little.

> Let me not hurt, by any selfish deed
> Or thoughtless word, the heart of foe or friend;
> Nor would I pass, unseeing, worthy need,
> Or sin by silence, when I should defend.

Another sigh escaped him. The shock that had landed on his chest, like a dark, murky splodge, lifted a little more.

> However meager be my worldly wealth,
> Let me give something that shall aid my kind -
> A word of courage, or a thought of health,
> Dropped as I pass for troubled hearts to find.

UNCLE JOSEPH'S TOOL BOX

Uncle Joseph found himself in a quandary: just how to act? He could not do it for the thief - *that* would be out of the question! But then, there was the man's wife. Her life would be ruined if her husband were to be imprisoned.

Although he never talked about his own deeds Uncle was, in fact, passionate about giving - which did not, however, provide him with much comfort in this instance! So he forced his mind back to his *Morning Prayer.*

> Let me to-night look back across the span
> 'Twixt dawn and dark, and to my conscience say
> Because of some good act to beast or man -
> "The world is better that I lived to-day."

Aunty and Uncle lived simple, frugal, and unassuming lives. They were economical in all things, and wasted nothing. Like her husband, Aunty had started life poor. Her mother had died three months after she was born, and her father a few years later. A loving stepmother had raised her and her brother (my father) alone on her meager teacher's pay. The memory of Necessity had remained branded into both Aunty and Uncle.

"When you have been *that* poor, you never forget it!"

Uncle would not speculate; nor take risks. Once a relative asked him for a loan to build a block of flats in Australia - with the assurance of guaranteed profit. He refused.

Not long afterwards the property boom ended, plunging many into long-term debt.

Now Uncle Joseph turned his *Morning Prayer* card over, and studied the back.

Be calm, serene, positive.

Behind every appearance of calamity
There is good, and by your faith you will
Bring it into evidence.

He breathed another sigh, straightened, shook off the last remnants of shock, and the shadow of that dark, murky splodge on his chest dissolved.

When Aymone phoned later that morning, Uncle Joseph said,
"Tell him to come to see me."

In time Mr. Le Roy repaid every centime, and his employer gave him another chance.

UNCLE JOSEPH'S TOOL BOX

Uncle loved telling me stories from his life. But all he ever said about this event - oh so quietly and just in passing - was,

"Once I was asked to lend money to a thief."

What's Important is the Rose

A girl accompanies an old man. Her thick, curly hair is burnished auburn in the sun. Tenderly he places his hand in hers. She takes it, and slows her pace. She is on holiday with her Uncle Joseph on the French Riviera and they are out on their morning walk.

He is wearing a ring today. The plain silver band embraces a tiny amethyst. It is the hour of violet. I fall in easily with the small, measured footsteps. We pass in front of the ochre villa with its overhanging wisteria in full bloom. Its sweet scent fills the air. The bees buzz gently.

We walk in comfortable silence; I in my thoughts, and he in his. We are passing the olive grove. The oblong, pointed leaves shimmer silvery-grey as they ripple in the breeze.

"This is where the Count used to live," he says, indicating a castle turned into a hotel.

We walk on. I feel Uncle's soft hand, its gentle strength. The cloudless sky covers us with its blue dome. The street shimmers in the sun, like fallen star-crystal. Despite his years, he carries himself erect, as might a young lord. I admire him; I tell him so.

"Don't go by appearances, Young One," he replies, warding off the admiration.

I feel the familiar pressure of his hand as he holds mine. His inner smile encompasses me. How I love those kind eyes, that vibrant stillness, that radiant peace.

We continue as one in silence; my steps as old as his. We pass a row of cypress trees that stand like sentinels along the way. I press my face into one and take a deep breath. Uncle picks a few cones and puts them into his bag. Back in his study, he will lay them out to dry on the maroon ceramic wood stove. They will add their scent to that of the little squares of paper impregnated with a few drops of aromatic oils he has placed in each corner of the room. For me, the fragrance of this room was sheer bliss.

Uncle turns right. My hand melds into his. We are still only half way on the outward walk. It is already half past eleven. Clouds have blown in, as if from nowhere. The sky, so clear when we left, becomes overcast.

A smile lights up his eyes and takes root in my heart. It swells within me. I need not look at my Uncle; I need not smile back.

As I fall in with the rhythmic step of the old man, his smile grows within me, expands me. I am becoming taller, taller, pushing through the barrier of cloud that now completely covers the sky. Suddenly my head emerges in the sun. I see him standing there beside me, as tall as I. And it is up there in the sun, the earth far below, that we recognize each other and exchange a smile. Two colossi, unbound from time, striding through space. My heart is in his, and his heart heals mine.

Once again, we are late for lunch.

After a long while Uncle says, "I wonder what will become of my wife when I am no longer here."

"I will look after her, I promise."

"Never make promises," he says earnestly. "One cannot know what life will bring."

"But I do promise, and I will."

In the years that followed, I was only able to visit my Uncle twice more. And without my having been aware of how quickly time had passed, Uncle had turned ninety-four.

When his time came, I was in South Africa with my two sons, on a three-month's visit to my father, who was seventy-two. I look back: it has been a joyful reunion.

My father looks much younger, and has great vitality and enthusiasm for life. He loves his work as consultant engineer, and has no thought of retirement. The three months could not have been more perfect. But they are coming to an end.

Back on the *Côte d'Azur,* Uncle has returned from the clinic where he spent three months with a broken thigh bone. Aunty took him his meals every day. Now he has been back home for a few days. Exhausted, he lies down.

Aunty is out: she has gone to the Opera.

The live-in maid has prepared dinner. But at eight o'clock Uncle does not come to the dining room as usual. She knocks at his door, and looks in. She sees him lying on the bed and knows that something has happened. As Aunty is out, the maid phones Aymone, and asks her to come. Aymone leaves at once, taking her daughter with her. Aunty will have to be paged.

By the time they arrive, Uncle is up and dressed.

At the same time in South Africa, my father has suddenly collapsed at work with a cerebral hemorrhage. For six days he has been in hospital in a coma, as if sleeping peacefully.

The members of the family have arrived from near and far. We stand around his bed on the seventh day, in silence. A few minutes after midday there is a loud clap of thunder, and my father's spirit leaves his body.

That evening we are too tired to make the long-distance call to Aunty and Uncle. So they do not know that my father has died; nor are we, so far away in South Africa, aware that Uncle Joseph is close to his own end.

But the next morning in the south of France, a whole continent away, Uncle Joseph sits up in bed, twice calls out my father's name - and cries out, "I'm coming!"

Then he steps out into Space.

They left the earth together.

Uncle's death, just twenty-four hours after my father's, left me desolate and bereft.

Aymone became my soul mother - for the rest of my days.

Later she told me, "Before he died, *Monsieur* said a few personal words to my daughter and me individually.

"Then, looking at us both, he said:

'My life is the message I leave you.'"

The years have gone by. How I wish Uncle had written a book.

But Aymone said: "Your Uncle was fifty years ahead of his time."

In their work together Uncle had filled fifteen notebooks. They were to be given to Aymone after his death. But instead Aunty took them to a disused quarry in the hills and burnt them.

It has taken my aunt years to come to terms with Uncle's death. She has given away his clothes, and one pair of boots. Now Aunty begins to give away some of his personal belongings. One holiday she gives me Uncle's green and white striped fountain-pen in its bottle-green leather case. And his little box of dull grey rings. There are seven, each with a tiny gemstone.

"Take them," she says. "They have no value."

Oh! But they do, to me!

Aunty gives me the spare pendulum; not the one that Uncle always used. *That* she has given away already, I don't know to whom, but not to Aymone. I carry the treasures home, like a magpie to its nest. Now I have Uncle's pen; I have his spare pendulum; I have his rings. I am rich beyond measure.

But all is not well with me. I have fallen into darkness. Grief holds me mercilessly. The loss is unbearable. I am unable to move on.

Aymone tells me, *"Le passé est matière morte.* The past is dead matter. It prevents one from living fully in the present. You must let go. Release the things that once belonged to your Uncle; there is no life in them now. Bury them in the earth or at sea."

No, no, no!
That is all I have left of him.
Not yet! Not yet!

I cling to the little objects that once were Uncle's as if my life depended on it. A year later friends invite me to spend a holiday with them in Portugal. They have a cottage in a hamlet somewhere North of Lisbon. I cannot avoid the issue any longer. The moment to decide has come. Yes, in Portugal! That's where I will *do it!*

I pack my Uncle-treasures and take them with me. The hamlet is inland, about fifty kilometers from the coast. A rural road leads to their low 18th century national heritage cottage. The beds are so short that my feet stick out at the end. We spend a pleasant week together.

Then, one day, towards the end of the holiday, I ask the young man of the house to take me to the sea. He has a rattling old van, and drives me along the wild coastline to a beautiful spot high above the sea. There is no beach; only a range of black rocks that wall the water.

My heart throbbing, I climb the sharp rocks barefoot, my treasures hidden in a bag.

The time has come to let go. I want no

questions; no eyes to watch. I plant my feet firmly on a rock, and gaze out into the sea, pretending to daydream. The young man lies back in the sun, and closes his eyes. I watch the sea pounding and the spray rising against the rocks.

Then, giving myself no time to think, I stretch my arm out and drop the bottle-green leather pen case into the water. The ocean plays with it, letting it float like a small skiff; then the waves wash it further and further out, till it disappears. Next, the fountain-pen.

How I had loved to see that pen in Uncle's hand!

Uncle had treated it with much appreciation, like a friend. The nib had broken once, but Uncle had had the pen repaired. There was no question, for him, of abandoning this faithful servant. And indeed, this pen had continued to serve him well, not only for his correspondence, all hand-written, but to fill the fifteen notebooks with his personal research.

Now the silver trimmings over the green and white stripes on black lacquered resin glisten in the sun.

Proud to receive it, proud to hold it, I had

also tried to write with it, but the words came out thick and smudgy. One cannot easily use a pen that has been polished to the cadence of another. Uncle had very fine handwriting, in a style uniquely his own. To produce such a fine script, he wrote with the topside of the nib.

I remove the pendulum from the black velvet pouch and drop it into the surging, rock-edge sea. It fills like a soggy bubble, bobs up and down for a while and is washed away. Before temptation gets the better of me, I fling the pendulum as far as I can out into the swirling water. Then I step back on the black rock, while the young man goes on sleeping.

That leaves me with the little box of rings. I take the rings out, and let the box fall into the water. It becomes warped, turns black, and sinks. I hold the rings in my hand. They are the closest I can get to Uncle. Each ring has a tiny, plain gemstone; each of a different color. The bands are a dull, dead grey. They no longer feel like Uncle or hold his energy. Leaving myself no time for regrets, I begin to let them go. One by one I fling them out into the ocean. They skip over the waves, then sink. Then there is only one left.

But no! I cannot let the last one go; it is Uncle's amethyst ring. I cannot live without it.

I see it all again now, how that last time, this ring had suddenly come alive, when Uncle and I had walked hand in hand, our feet on the earth, and our heads in the sun.

How I miss those walks!

Lost thus in my perplexity, I hear the young man's voice at last, "We must be getting back."

The sun is beginning to set; the wind has come up sharply, whipping the blue-grey waters, and the coastline looks lonely and wild. Uncle's pen has dived down, the rings have been washed away, and the pendulum has sunk. The ocean has taken all into itself. I gather up my things and get back into the battered van. My hand is surprised to find itself clutching its single treasure.

As we drive the thirty kilometers back to the cottage in which I have spent a happy week, I slip the amethyst ring onto my thumb. It is far too big. I twist it round and round. A point begins to brighten on the long-dulled silver. I rub it with the edge of my skirt as the young man drives on.

Look! The ring is coming alive. I will keep it; keep it close to me. I must have it. My life depends on it.

The vacation has drawn to a close. On the last day I set out towards the hills, and stop at the ancient olive grove. Some trees grow straight, some are crooked or bent. I feel at home in its familiar blue-green haze. At one end lies the olive press, resting in the sun. I imagine the heavy millstone rolling in a circle over the olives in the large stone basin, for half of each olive is oil. But there will be no more harvests here. I stroll along the alley between the trees, and touch the grey bark of the gnarled trunks, now this one, now that.

How I miss Uncle

"I inherited the olive grove from my father," my hostess had told me. "The trees are over three hundred years old and no longer bear fruit. But I decided to let them be."

As I walk past the trees, I run my fingers lightly over their leaves, ruffling them tenderly, and watch them shimmer silvery-grey in the sun, as they did back then, when Uncle and I would pass the olive grove on our morning walks.

I clutch my last treasure as one who is drowning. I feel its caress. But I hear Aymone repeat: *Release the past. Let go and live.*

I press the ring to my lips. Then I drop it into the hollow bole of a gnarled and twisted olive tree, and hear it land.

I often think back to that holiday in Portugal, and how the great blue-grey water had embraced the treasures that once belonged to the Uncle I loved, and had taken them unto itself. No hand had risen out of the waters to catch, but the vast blue-grey ocean had laid them to rest.

The years have added themselves to the girl I then was, as *I* became *we*, and *we* became *three*, then *four*. I no longer remember the name of that hamlet north of Lisbon, and I have forgotten how to get there. But still I know that somewhere, down a country path that ends in scrub at the foot of a hill, is an ancient olive grove.

There, deep in the bole of a wild olive tree, twisted and gnarled with age, lies an amethyst ring that once belonged to a mortal who had walked with me so often, hand in hand - my young one in his, his old one in mine - feet on the earth and head in the sun.

About the Author

Sophia Tellen is a student of Life, committed to the search for Truth. She explores the experiences of her life as she moves in and out of countries and cultures, experiences change and meets the challenge of jobs high and low, professional and laic, while becoming a wife, mother, and finally writer. She now gives back and shares the insights and blessings that have accompanied her on her journey.